Nell and the Girls

Nell and the Girls

The True Story of a British Girl and her Family
in Occupied France 1940–1944

Jeanne Gask

MYRMIDON

Myrmidon
Rotterdam House
116 Quayside
Newcastle upon Tyne
NE1 3DY

www.myrmidonbooks.com
Published by Myrmidon 2015

A catalogue record for this book is available from the British Library.

ISBN 978-1-910183-11-3

Set in Fournier MT by
Ellipsis Digital Limited, Glasgow

Printed and bound in the UK by
CPI Group (UK) Ltd, Croydon, CR0 4YY

1 3 5 7 9 10 8 6 4 2

In memory of Nell, and for all women like her.

Contents

About the Author

Jeanne Elisabeth Gask was born in Calais, the youngest daughter of a British family living and working in France at the time of its fall and occupation in 1940. As a British citizen, her father was interned by the SS and the family was left to fend for itself for the duration of the war.

After Liberation they returned to join their family in Birmingham and Jeanne finished her education. She married Tony, a typographer, in the mid-1950s and they had three daughters, just like her parents. Home was in Teddington, Middlesex, then Manchester, with Jeanne staying home to bring up the girls. Later the couple moved to Bristol where Jeanne had a thoroughly enjoyable time as a French-speaking, blue-badge Bath and Bristol tourist guide.

In recent years she attended a Creative Writing group in Bristol and told her tutors she wanted to write a book about her early life in France. They showed her how to get started and followed her progress right through. The result is *Nell and the Girls*.

Jeanne is passionate about travel. She is a great fan of the music of Edith Piaf and Charles Trenet and belongs to a film club showing old French films. Tony and Jeanne bought a second home in the Charente area of France some twenty years ago, and Jeanne likes to feel she has a foot in each country. She has five grandchildren and lives with Tony in Teddington, Middlesex.

To this day Jeanne always makes the sign of a cross on every new loaf *so that we'll never want for bread*, a superstition she learnt from her stoical mother, Nell.

Prologue: March 1940

Tom came home with five identical square boxes.

'Now then you three, line up!'

He called out, 'Nell, come in here a minute, we're going to try our gasmasks on!' Out of the boxes came the most horrible, grotesque apparitions, straight out of Jeanne's worst nightmares. She was stiff with terror. Tom, Nell and her sisters tried theirs on. Tom, wearing the fearsome mask, brought his face right down to Jeanne's level.

'Now, come on Jeannot, be reasonable. Don't be a silly girl!' His voice came out of the mask, thin and muffled, and making the most awful sound when he took his breath in, just like Sandy next door when his asthma was playing him up.

Jeanne sobbed, frightened. 'No, no . . . I can't. I'm scared . . . I won't be able to breathe.'

Tom was angry now. 'Come on, don't be stupid! You can see we're all wearing them and we can all breathe.'

Panic set in. Jeanne gave full vent to her hysteria. She

opened her mouth wide. 'Wa-a-a-gh!'

Tom lunged towards her, her way of escape into the hall cut off by hands trying to grab hold of her. There was only one thing for it – quick! – behind the piano. As luck would have it, the piano had been placed at an angle across the corner of the room. She squeezed in and curled herself up into a very tight ball. Tom could not get hold of her, either from the side or from the top. Her sisters, Marie and Irene, giggled eerily somewhere deep inside their gasmasks.

Tom took off his mask and threw it to the ground. 'Oh, I give up. That child's becoming impossible, Nell.' As though it was Nell's fault.

Jeanne stayed curled up in her haven behind the piano, quietly sobbing to herself until it was safe to come out.

1890 – 1940

1. Tom

William 'Bill' Simpson Sarginson and his friend Willie Peacock left Penrith, Cumberland, in the early 1890s to seek their fortunes. They were both tailors at a time when British materials and tailoring were much sought after.

Bill was soon employed as First Cutter by the prestigious House of Worth in Paris. He married Jeanne Marie-Francoise Tirefort, a *giletiere* (waistcoat maker) and they had two children, Marguerite 'Maggie', born in 1894, and Tom, born in 1896.

When Tom was baptised, the Catholic priest refused to name him Tom as it was not a saint's name but said that Thomas would do. Bill insisted that he wanted the child named Tom after his uncle back in Penrith. The priest agreed, but only if the boy also had another name, that of a saint. Bill and Jeanne thought quickly, and so the boy was named Tom Paul, after the acceptable name of a saint. Bill had Tom registered as a British citizen at the British Consulate in Paris.

The family lived in a flat in central Paris: 22, rue Cler in the shadow of Les Invalides.

Bill had a workshop where he had a full-scale model of a horse, as he specialised in ladies' riding habits *en amazone* – meaning side-saddle, to ride in the Bois de Boulogne. The model enabled him to drape the habit to his satisfaction and the children were allowed to ride on the horse when they visited occasionally. On one of their visits they met one of Bill's clients, a Belgian princess who entertained the children by letting her jewel-encrusted pet scarab beetle run up and down the mantelpiece much to their delight.

While in Paris, young Tom was taken to see Buffalo Bill's Wild West Show. What a treat that was for a boy, he was most struck by the Whirling Dervishes, one on each corner of the showground, who, he said, never stopped spinning for the whole four hours. He also saw *La Goulue*, the dancer depicted dancing on Toulouse-Lautrec's famous posters of the *Moulin Rouge*. She had become known as the 'Queen of Paris' but, by the time Tom saw her exhibited in a lion's cage in a circus show, she was old and well past her glory days.

When the children were in their early teens, Bill was promoted to manager of Old England, an establishment promoting British tailoring in Brussels, and the whole family moved there. They lived in rue de l'Arbre Beni, Ixelles, a suburb of Brussels.

Maggie was apprenticed to a leading Belgian milliner and was to make the rosettes for the wedding bonnet of the Belgian Princess Marie-Jose who married the Italian Crown Prince.

Bill had advised Tom to go into Electricity. 'That's where the future is, my boy.' And so, in 1912, Tom was apprenticed to a Swiss firm in Brussels, Appareillage Gardy, learning about high and low tension switchgear.

When the Germans invaded Belgium in 1914, Tom and Bill were arrested and taken to the Ecole Militaire together with other British subjects at the end of August 1914. Bill, observing the comings and goings of crowds of people, all seeking help or information of some sort or other, said to Tom, 'Look, I think we can escape. Just follow me, don't look right nor left.' And that's exactly what they did. They threaded their way through the crowd looking neither right nor left, and found themselves back in the street and free.

They couldn't go home and so stayed with kind friends: Bill at one house and Tom at another. They met Jeanne and Maggie, who were still free, at church on Sundays or in the park to exchange news and washing. Jeanne and Maggie were repatriated to England soon after by the Americans who were not yet in the war.

When a decree was issued that anyone sheltering British subjects would be shot, Bill decided that it was time to escape, as they didn't want to put their friends in danger. It is thought that they were helped by the Edith Cavell organisation; although this is not certain and records no longer exist, her hospital was also in the Ixelles district of Brussels.

Bill and Tom took a tram all the way to the terminus towards the Dutch border and then started to walk. They were helped through the Dutch marshes and over the border by tobacco smugglers, who were paid for their trouble. They were now free and in neutral Holland. With very little money left, they made their way to the British Consulate and were given places on a Dutch fishing boat. On the way over, they narrowly missed a mine and finally landed in England on January 13th 1915.

They were grilled by the authorities in London for a fortnight to make sure of their identity and were fed, clothed and given work by the Salvation Army, for whom Tom retained a lifelong gratitude.

When the authorities allowed them to go, they made their way up to Penrith. Bill got work in Barrow-in-Furness, and Tom working on electrical maintenance in Carr's Biscuit Factory in Carlisle. However, it was not long before Tom was longing for more excitement and enlisted. He joined up on June 22nd 1915.

He found himself in Farnborough doing his basic training in the uniform of the Royal Flying Corps (forerunner of the RAF) still knowing very little English.

The widow of the exiled Napoleon III, Empress Eugenie, lived nearby in a large house on Farnborough Hill and had opened part of it to be used as a hospital for wounded officers. She would attend church parade every Sunday at the training camp and would send for *Mon Petit Francais*, her little Frenchman, and Tom would go forward and respectfully have a chat with her.

After training, Tom was on the move again. Jeanne and Maggie came to say goodbye to him and he was sent back to France. He found himself in Pont de L'Arche, near Rouen, working on the maintenance of planes and transport. He was billeted with Monsieur and Madame Desrue, owners of the village grocery shop, and enjoyed helping out in the shop on his free days, sometimes being left completely in charge. He remained friends with the couple for many years.

When demobbed, he came back to England and completed his apprenticeship at Trafford Park, Manchester, under an ex-servicemen's scheme. He then worked at various firms, always bettering himself, until he landed up in Birmingham as foreman at a lighting and power installations firm. He asked one of the typists to type a letter in French for him and bought her a box of chocolates. Then he took her to the pictures. One of the typists cousins soon reported to her parents that she had been seen at he pictures with 'that Frenchman'. The typist's name was Frances Helen Lewis, known as 'Nell'.

Nell's was Birmingham born and bred. Her parents were of the 'poor but honest' school of upbringing. Nell recalled that, when she was young in Handsworth, the family kept two jars above the mantelpiece that a few coins went into each and every payday: one was for coal and the other for a holiday – always taken in Aberystwyth. They were the only family in their street to have a holiday every year.

Eventually, Nell's father, Percy John Lewis, obtained a small workshop in the Jewellery District of Birmingham, stamping locks and hinges for jewellery boxes. He employed half-a-dozen women until World War II, when most left for better paid work in munitions. He carried on until the 1960s and retired when he was eighty-five.

Nell's family were deeply religious: when Nell as a young girl was paying the piano her aunts, who had come to tea, discussed at length if she should be allowed such entertainment on a Sunday, but decided it was permissible as the child was playing hymns. Nell had a fondness for music and, just before she met Tom, had joined a local amateur singing group: 'The Blackbirds'.

Tom and Nell married on 31st May 1924.

2. The Good Days

Tom was a happy man. Back in England, during the depression of the late 1920s / early 1930s, he had answered an advertisement in the employment columns of an English newspaper. Staff were required for the new Courtaulds factory at Calais in northern France. As Tom was now a trained electrician and French was his mother tongue he was a natural choice for the position of Chief Electrical Engineer. He moved over to Calais early in 1927 to help get the new factory off the ground and Nell and his baby daughter Beatrice Marie followed close behind.

The furthest Nell had ever been from home was for the yearly holiday to Aberystwyth in Wales. And now she had followed Tom to a foreign land not knowing a word of French. She felt quite apprehensive about the whole thing.

A row of English-style houses was built for the foremen of the new factory and Tom and Nell moved into one of them. There, Irene Marguerite was born in 1928 and Jeanne Elisabeth in 1932. The family was now complete and the girls were brought up in relative luxury. Nell found herself with both a live-in maid and a cleaning lady. When they were old enough, Nell drove the girls to the Lycee every day, the College Sophie Berthelot in Calais. By 1939, Marie, aged thirteen, was already an accomplished pianist. An examiner had told her at the age of nine that she was gifted. She had not known what that meant; she thought she had done badly! Irene, aged eleven, loved her violin lessons, and there was talk of Jeanne joining a choir.

Clothilde, the maid, would come into Jeanne's bedroom every winter's morning carrying a basket. As Jeanne watched, with bedclothes scratching her chin and Dick their dog lying on her feet, the maid crumpled up sheets of old newspaper and laid them in the fireplace. She next criss-crossed the sticks of wood over the paper and finally placed some chunks of coal over the top.

Then she lit the paper with a match and Jeanne looked on fascinated as the wood spat and crackled. When the coal was glowing red and warm, she knew she could get up and dress in front of the fire, ready for school.

Tom and Nell led an exciting social life. Jeanne used to think her Mummy looked every bit a princess in her beautiful long dresses when she came to kiss her goodnight. What she didn't know was that Tom and Nell sang duets on one of the very first commercial stations, Radio Normandie, run by British enthusiasts and based in Fecamp, a little way down the coast. The station broadcast across to England, where commercial radio was illegal.

When her parents held a dinner party, Tom would order two-dozen oysters and spend a frantic half hour before the guests arrived, prising the obstinate shells with a small, sharp knife. All his choicest Royal Flying Corps language came out during these sessions and Jeanne was sent out of the kitchen until he had finished. She was allowed downstairs later and, sitting on a guest's knee at the dinner table, was allowed a sip or two from their glass of wine before being sent back to bed.

The garden was Jeanne's domain. With Leon, the boy next door, she was constantly busy on the swing, in the sandpit and in the field at the back of the houses. There was always so much to do and so much mischief to get up to.

One particular time, she and Leon got drunk. The episode was evermore known in the family's history as *The Story of the Kummel Bottle*. She and Leon were rummaging about on an old rubbish tip in the back field one sunny afternoon. They found an empty bottle of Kummel, the delicious damson liqueur from eastern France. Noticing there was some crystallised sugar left in the bottom of the bottle they smashed it on a rock and, with a sharp stone, prised the hardened, liqueur-soaked sugar from the pieces of glass and ate it. The more they ate the more unwell they felt. They came home swaying and complaining of headaches. After a stiff questioning by anxious parents, they were sent to bed to sleep it off, to everyone's great amusement. In future, whenever someone wanted to embarrass her, they would say, 'Remember the Kummel story, Jeanne?' She would slink away, her face bright red, remembering something she needed to do urgently.

As well as Dick the dog, there was Zezette, the beautiful black and white cat, and one day, to Jeanne's delight, Tom brought home a dozen chicks. He built an incubator with a light burning night and day. He explained that it was to keep the chicks warm and to pretend it was the mother hen. The girls named every one of the chicks. There was Popov, an East European politician forever being mentioned on the radio; Daladier, the French prime minister; and the stripy one they called Zebraline.

Tradesmen called at the house. 'Grandpere Cresson' sold freshly-gathered watercress door-to-door, and fishermen brought their catch to the front door. Jeanne liked Monsieur and Madame Matelas best of all. Well that's what they called them; they never knew their real names. They came once a year and took over the garage, emptied for the purpose. They set up a large trestle table and spent the day bringing the mattresses down from the bedrooms, one by one, unpicking them down one side, and taking the wool out. Jeanne liked to watch them; it was an event to look forward to. The floor of the garage spread with large, clean sheets was completely covered with tight wads of wool, like an Australian sheepshearers' shed. Monsieur and Madame took great armfuls of wool and fluffed it up, letting the air get at it. They then returned the wool to the mattress, adding more if it was needed, and stitched the side up. When the job was done to their satisfaction, they took the finished mattress upstairs, brought another one down and started all over again. It took up the whole day.

Tom and Nell would rent a seaside cottage at Sandgatte, outside Calais, and the whole household, including Clothilde the maid, would spend the summer months there. Tom commuted to work every day in his beloved Maigret-style Citroën.

The cottage backed onto the beach. It was paradise for three young girls. Jeanne had a shrimping net and spent hours in the shallows with Dick the dog catching shrimps, an assortment of shells and the occasional crab. She learned early to keep away from jellyfish that abounded on the beach but admired their wonderful colours from afar.

Gramp, Granny and Nell's sister Elsie, known as Rikkie, came over from England. There were long family days and beach picnics.

Yes, life was good to Tom, Nell and the girls, but all that was to change on September 3rd, 1939.

The First World War, called 'the war to end all wars', had left the whole of Europe in turmoil, not least vanquished Germany. When Hitler became German Chancellor in the early 1930s, he was thought by many to be the saviour of the German nation. He began regenerating the depressed German economy and building motorways, cars and planes, giving hope to the conquered people.

But almost from the start, he was looking beyond the German frontiers. He annexed Austria, Bohemia and Moravia and, to a mixed reception, his troops entered Prague, the Czechoslovak capital, in March 1939.

He next laid claim to Danzig (Gdansk) in Poland. Britain and France had pledged to defend Poland. On 22nd August 1939, Hitler announced the destruction of Poland 'starting on Saturday morning'. German troops entered Poland the next day. Britain and France gave Germany an ultimatum to withdraw from Poland by 11.00 am on 3rd September, or war would be declared on Germany. At 11.15 am on that day Neville Chamberlain, the British Prime Minister, made his famous broadcast, saying that, 'No such undertaking has been received, and consequently this country is at war with Germany.'

At first, life went on much as before. This is the period known as the 'phoney war'. Tom carried on working, and the girls returned to the college Sophie Berthelot at the end of the summer holidays.

Then, almost imperceptibly, things started to change.

'Look, Jeannot,' Nell said one evening, 'I've decided to take you away from the college. You'll have to go to the local school.'

Jeanne was offended. 'But it's full of children I'm not allowed to play with. Those awful Durie children go there. Pooh . . . they smell . . . I don't want to go there . . . Don't let me go there . . . I don't want to go . . . Why can't I carry on going to the college? Why Mummy, why?'

'I'm sorry Jeannot, there's nothing I can do about it. I can't get hold of enough petrol to drive you girls to college any more. Marie and Irene can walk there, but you're too young. It's too far. You'll have to go to the village school.'

And that was that.

Then an anti-aircraft battery appeared in the field at the back of the house. It became a meeting place for all the children of the neighbourhood. They spent their time bothering the gun crew and being chased off. Jeanne was learning a few choice words she had never heard before and behaviour that would not have been acceptable previously. Her real education had begun in earnest.

As Spring came, events began hotting up. The grown-ups were getting more and more boring, shushing Jeanne whenever the radio news came on. There was talk of the Maginot Line, the British Expeditionary Forces pouring into France, someone called Mr Chamberlain forever attending meetings. None of it made sense to her.

Tom and Nell were constantly in a huddle, holding long, whispered conversations and telling Jeanne to 'go and play'.

Still . . . Jeanne had something else to think about; something far more exciting. Her birthday was near. She would be eight on May 10th. Imagine . . . eight – why, that was almost grown up! She knew exactly what she wanted for her birthday. Dolls were not for her; dolls were cissy, stupid things. No, she asked for something much better: tin soldiers, and preferably British ones. A week before the great day, Nell took her to town to choose her present. And there they all were in the shop window, exactly as she had pictured them: a squad of nine British soldiers, in full battle khaki with tin hats on, marching proudly into battle in three rows of three. In front, the flag bearer held the Union Jack aloft, and behind, oh joy of joys, a gun that fired real caps. She was hopping up and down, first on one foot, then the other but, once Nell had bought them, she put the soldiers away.

'You'll get them on your birthday,' she promised.

One evening just before her birthday, Jeanne heard a commotion downstairs. Looking through the banister railings, she saw a man gesticulating and shouting excitedly.

'Monsieur Tom, Monsieur Tom, all the English are leaving. Go, you must go, the last boat is leaving for Dover tonight!'

'No,' Tom said, adamant. 'My place is here with my work. I'm not going.' He called to Nell as he closed the door. 'They're fools, they're all panicking. It'll all be over in no time. It'll be over by Christmas. You'll see.'

1940 – 1941

3. The Balloon Goes Up

'Not even my soldiers?' Jeanne was incredulous.

'No, there's no room in the car. We're just taking bare essentials.' Realising the unfairness of it all to a just-eight year old, Nell gave her a hug. 'I'm sorry, Jeannot, we'll make it up to you later, see if we won't.'

On the morning of May 10th, all hell had let loose, the birthday completely forgotten, overtaken by momentous events. During the night, German troops had invaded and overrun Holland then neutral Belgium. The war had started in earnest. Hordes of refugees poured over the border into France, carrying what possessions they could in cars, lorries, horse-drawn carts, handcarts, bikes, on foot; all fleeing in front of the enemy in a chaotic rabble.

Tom held a family conference. 'We'll go camping. We'll go south. You girls remember how much you enjoyed it down in Provence. You'll see. It'll be fun. And it won't last long, it'll just be a long holiday, longer than usual.'

Clothilde the maid was sent home to her parents in floods

of tears. Dick the dog, Zezette the cat and the chicks were taken to friends in the country. 'It won't be for long. We'll pick them up on our return.'

Tom strapped two double mattresses, one on top of the other, to the car roof for the gruesome purpose of protecting them from machine-gun bullets. He tied the old canvas tent to the rear bumper, put clothes and food in the boot. Once the three girls were on the back seat, he locked up the house and they set off.

They suffered a horrendous journey.

Almost immediately, their progress was slowed down. They had become part of the great exodus of refugees, all fleeing south, away from the approaching German troops. Jeanne knew what refugees were as she had seen some in a camp on the beach outside Calais just two years before. Nell had told her that they were Spanish refugees from the Civil War and Jeanne had felt sorry for the barefoot children.

They reached Abbeville during the night to find the town in flames and their way blocked. They had only driven seventy-five miles and it was impossible to cross the river Somme. Nell looked at the map with a torch.

'We can cross at St Valery, further up. There's a bridge there. Go back to sleep, Jeanne, there's a good girl.'

Dawn found all the refugees being diverted off the road into a field.

'It's to make way for a column of French tanks. They're expected...'

'That'll show 'em!' People were smiling, cheered up.

'Let's chase the Boches back over the Maginot Line and then we can all go home,' they said.

Towards lunchtime the refugees were back on the road. There were no tanks.

Tom was still trying to make his way to St Valery so that they might cross the river there. They met a British Army ambulance full of wounded going in the opposite direction. They stopped and exchanged information with the driver and the nurses. It became obvious they were going round in circles.

'Come on,' Tom said, grimly. 'We'll still try for the bridge.'

But just a few hundred yards on, a French soldier with a rifle in his hand waved them down urgently. 'Get out! Get down into the ditch, quick . . . quick . . .!'

They tumbled out of the car, ran into a small wood, and lay down as they had been told, joining other refugees there. A machine-gun rat-tat-tat-ted fifty yards away.

The soldier shouted to Nell, 'Don't worry about your fur-coat, Madame! Get right down . . . flat!'

After some time, the panic was averted and they were allowed to carry on, but where to?

Tom turned to Nell and the girls. 'Look, I'm sorry. We're trapped. We're exhausted. Let's find some shelter for the night. When the French troops have kicked the Germans out of the area, we'll drive on.'

They knocked on the door of the nearest farmhouse, begging shelter for the night. The farmyard was overflowing with refugees.

The farmer was sceptical. 'Well . . . I don't know. We're packed out.' He stroked his chin thoughtfully. His farmyard was full to bursting: French, Belgians and Dutch refugees living in his yard, sleeping in his barn. But he took pity on the tired family.

'Oh, all right then, but you're the last. You can sleep over there, with the others.'

Jeanne woke the next morning to find a hen scratching for food in the straw right by her head. She had never been on a farm before and she was thrilled. She prodded her sisters awake. They picked the bits of straw out of each other's clothes and hair and looked for their parents.

Tom and Nell were already talking to the farmer, poking about and wandering in and out of stables and outhouses. What on earth were they doing?

Tom came over to the girls.

'The farmer's let us have an empty cowshed. When Mum and I have cleaned it out, we can sleep in it.'

Jeanne was sorry they wouldn't be sleeping in the barn again; she'd liked that.

The girls set off to explore their new surroundings. The farmyard was full of people trying to get over their ordeal, washing themselves, washing clothes and feeding children. A flurry of domesticity, all in the open air. A gang of five lads from Lille, speaking their northern dialect, had killed a hare, skinned it and were cooking it in a pot on a makeshift fire set up in the middle of the yard. The children were hanging around, attracted by the aroma, hoping for a mouthful to come their way.

The girls made everyone's acquaintance, found children of their own age who took them to see the farm animals. Jeanne was in heaven; she did so love animals.

The sisters and their newfound friends kept popping back to the cowshed to check on Tom and Nell's progress.

Finally, in the early evening, Tom said, 'All right, the floor's dry now. You girls can help me get the mattresses in.'

He un-strapped them from the car roof and they carried them in one at a time to lay them ceremoniously side by side on the stone floor. Nell followed in with the tiny camping stove to make a kitchen of sorts.

The girls bounced up and down on the mattresses, giggling delightedly. They lay down and found their new home to their liking. Marie pointed out a swallow's nest high up in the eaves, and they watched as the parent birds flew in and out, feeding their noisy family.

Tom followed them in.

'Well,' he said, looking round him, 'it isn't exactly the Ritz, but it's an improvement on the barn!'

The next day the refugees staying on the farm, all twenty-four of them, stood in a row on the side of the road as the German troops rolled in. The gang of lads from Lille started to run away, but Tom shouted out, 'Don't run, they'll shoot you.' The boys stood still.

They were now 'occupied'.

A young German army officer stood in the middle of the field, flanked by two of his soldiers, surveying the assembled crowd. His orders were simple: try and calm the situation down. Be friendly. Try and put them at their ease. The people really did look frightened, backing away to the edges of the field as far away from him as possible.

He saw his soldiers mingling among them, offering sweets to the children. Many parents made them throw them away. There had been rumours about poisoned sweets. One soldier was comically unwrapping a sweet and putting it in his mouth, saying, '*Nein, nein . . . gut, gut!*'

The officer noticed a family standing a little apart. They looked different from the others: three blonde-headed little girls that could have been German; mother smart, fur-coated, and the father, defiant but scared, holding the hand of the youngest girl, who was peeping fearfully from behind him.

Jeanne, holding her Daddy's hand, was frightened. The big soldiers all had club-shaped grenades tucked into the top of their jackboots. Daddy had explained to her that you only had to pull the pin out of the grenade and you had ten seconds before it exploded. She eyed the grenades apprehensively.

The young officer shouted out, 'We have assembled you to count you. Report to the *Mairie* (Town Hall) daily. We will tell refugees when to go home. I want the French on the left of the field, and the Belgians and Dutch on the right.' The crowd parted, leaving Tom and his family isolated.

'Yes?' said the officer brusquely.

'I'm British.' Heart in mouth, Tom expected to be led to the nearest tree and shot.

'My goodness,' the officer said in perfect English. 'What are you doing here?' He thought for a moment. He didn't quite know what to do with them; his orders hadn't included stray English families. 'Oh well, you'd better go with the French.'

At this time, one of the most momentous episodes of the war was being enacted at Dunkirk, twenty-five miles north of Calais. The allied army was ordered to retreat to Dunkirk beach, where every available pleasure steamer, fishing boat, boats of all shapes and sizes, was coming over from Britain to rescue the beleaguered troops. They were being constantly shelled by the Germans. It was a highly hazardous operation. In all, 861 boats rescued 224,585 British and 112,546 French and Belgian servicemen and took them back to safety in England.

Of course Tom and Nell knew nothing of this and life for them was difficult enough. Tom reported to the *Mairie* every day and had to nearly fight for their ration of rock-hard, month-old bread. Food was in short supply.

After three weeks, empty houses and holiday villas were allocated to the refugees to stay in until it was safe to go home.

Tom and his family found themselves in a holiday villa in a nearby seaside town.

It was here that Jeanne was beaten up by a gang of local children, angry at her presence and defending their territorial rights. Eight or ten of them set on her, kicking and punching her with cries of, 'Go home, dirty refugee!' She ran home crying her eyes out and fell, sobbing, in Nell's lap.

'They won't play with me . . .' Jeanne was having to learn some very hard lessons.

On June 25th the French surrendered and a cease-fire began. Tom and his family were ordered home. They viewed the journey with dread, but apart from seeing a couple of dead bodies at the roadside, they got home safely.

Tom, Nell and the girls stood outside their house. They had been met by Madame Durie and Nell could see she was flustered, a red spot growing upon each cheek.

'But . . . We thought you'd gone back to England?' She kept them talking in the road. Tales of looters coming in droves across the fields, taking chairs, tables, whole three-piece suites, anything they could carry.

When they finally let themselves into the house, they found they too had been looted, the house was in turmoil. Tom and Nell stepped over the rubbish, what was left of their possessions, their home they had been so proud of, and tried to make out exactly what had been left by the looters. Casting an experienced housewife's eye over the rooms, Nell said, 'Someone's been in here quite recently, the dust is disturbed . . . Look, my silver tray's still moving!' And indeed it was. Nell's silver tray, a wedding present from her boss back in Birmingham, propped up on the mantelpiece behind the clock, was moving to and fro almost imperceptibly. Somebody had just left the house by the back door as the family entered by the front one. When Nell recounted this story in later years, she always swore that 'Pa' Durie had been busy replacing the objects he had stolen, while his wife kept Tom and Nell talking at the front. No wonder the woman had been so flustered.

Jeanne shouted, 'My soldiers! What about my soldiers?' She dashed up the stairs two at a time, into her bedroom and dived under the bed. Feeling along the struts under the springs, she found what she was looking for: her precious box of soldiers. Well, at least the looters had left them alone!

They tried to return to some kind of normality. Tom spent long hours at work, trying to formulate a working plan and the girls returned to school.

For once Jeanne was being good, not chattering or giggling but sitting at her school desk copying difficult words off the blackboard onto her slate while trying not to make the chalk squeak. She had been back at the village school a few days.

The headmistress burst into the room and whispered urgently to the teacher. The teacher pointed to the tallest girl in the class and said, 'You come here!' She whispered a few urgent instructions to the girl. Then, 'Jeanne Sarginson, come here!'

What have I done now? Jeanne thought, as she walked towards the teacher.

The teacher said to Jeanne, 'Go, run . . . run as fast as you can . . . run, little one, run . . .!'

The big girl took hold of Jeanne's hand and ran out of the school, across the playground and up the road. 'Come on, faster, faster!' she urged. Quick, quick . . . as fast as they could, up to the end of the road, round the corner, down a long, long road, miles long. But where were they going? And why in such a hurry? Jeanne hadn't even had time to take off her gingham school pinny and she had never worn it outside school. She felt quite embarrassed. It didn't feel right at all.

Still they ran on, the big girl egging her on. 'Come on, come on!'

Jeanne was puffing, breathless, and her legs were aching. They couldn't possibly carry her any further.

Just when she felt she couldn't run another step, she saw her Daddy in his long winter coat standing at the end of the road by a German army car. Next to him there was a German officer with a huge silver plaque across his chest.

'Papa . . . Daddy.' She hurled herself against him.

Tom bent down crying. He kissed his daughter and said, 'Goodbye, Jeannot. There's my good girl.'

The German got hold of his arm roughly and said, 'Come on!' They got in the car and sped away, leaving the two breathless, puzzled girls standing on the street corner staring where the car had been.

'What on earth was all that about? Why has my Daddy gone with that German?' It made no sense. It made no sense at all.

4. Departure Days

It only took Nell a matter of hours to find out where Tom was being held. All the British men in the area were being rounded up and locked up in Calais Town Hall. Nell went straight there that evening, but wasn't allowed to see Tom. She wasn't deterred. She would try again the next day.

'Come on, let's try and see Daddy today,' she said to the girls.

From that day on Nell's chin was tilted a little higher. There was an air of defiance about her and it stayed with her for the next four-and-a-half years.

The imposing Flemish-style Calais Town Hall stands alone in the town centre, a monument to civic pride. One might think it is very old but in fact it was only finished in 1926. Surrounded by formal gardens, the centrepiece is the magnificent bronze group, *The Six Burghers of Calais* by Rodin.

Back in 1346, Edward III of England, fresh from his

victory at nearby Crecy, laid siege to the town of Calais. The town was considered a valued prize for the English being the nearest point on the continent of Europe. After eleven months the starving *Calaisiens* were forced to request terms of surrender. Their six noblest citizens, the burghers, presented themselves to the English king in long shirts, barefoot, with the keys of the town around their necks. Edward III was for beheading them but Queen Philippa, his wife, fell to her knees and pleaded for their lives. The burghers were spared and the town was taken.

There they now stand, larger than life, caught by the sculptor in attitudes of submission and humility.

Going up the Town Hall steps, the visitor finds himself in the main entrance hall, and up the steps to the right, he comes to the first floor. On the left is a huge reception room extending along the whole frontage of the building but turning right is a smaller, longish room with an allegorical mural depicting *Spring* on the wall at the far end. This is the *Salle des Marriages*, the room in which the civil wedding ceremony following the church weddings are held. This is the room in which the British men were imprisoned. Incidentally, General Charles de Gaulle married his wife Yvonne Vendroux in this room.

Calais in 1940 had a sizeable British population. As well as the two British-owned firms, Courtaulds and Bramptons, there were port authority and customs employees as well as ex-servicemen employed by the British War Graves Commission keeping the First World War cemeteries manicure-tidy. There were also remnants from that war, ex-servicemen who had chosen not to go home to their wives and families after the armistice of 1918 and now had French 'wives' and children. All these men knew each other.

They now sat in a group and conjectured, questions coming more easily than answers. What would happen to them? They were all civilians; the Geneva Convention was there to protect them. How long would they be held here? Where would they all go? And their families, what would happen to them?

Then they would fall silent, each going through his own private hell.

Another conversation would start up: Had anyone seen old Bill since the invasion? Maybe he's got away? And a rueful cheer would go up as yet another victim was brought in.

At any time of day or night, little knots of relatives, friends and neighbours were to be seen, heads tilted backwards, exchanging news and information with the prisoners up at the windows. Nell and the girls went every day.

'What's the food like?' they called up to Tom. 'Are you getting enough to eat? Shall we bring you something?'

'No, no. Keep it for the girls. It's not as good as *Chez Marielles'* Sunday menu, but we can't grumble. No, don't bring anything. Keep it for the girls. Oh, Nell, can you go round to George's and tell his wife he needs his overcoat.'

'Tom, May's worried about Sandy's asthma . . .'

'Sandy's all right, don't worry. Tell her he's all right, we'll look after him.'

As the days went on Jeanne noticed a puzzling damp patch spreading below the left-hand window of the Salle des Marriages, each day getting wider and longer, until it eventually reached the ground. The smell was awful.

The men were peeing in the town of Calais' ceremonial dinner service and tipping it out of the window, just like medieval housewives!

On the tenth day, Nell was on her way to visit Tom yet again when she was held up at the level crossing at Gare des Fontinettes. A train was stopped in the station and, to her horror, she recognised some of the men looking out of the windows. She gasped. There was Sandy Youll, Reg Rainey and others. She ran out of the car, through the gate and along the platform calling 'Tom, Tom!' and there he was, squashed against the window like a sardine as there were too many men to a carriage. They held hands until the train pulled away, bound for an unknown destination.

Nell went straight on to the *Kommandantur* but could not get much information from the authorities. A few days later she was told, 'Report here in 24 hours. You are going to rejoin your men.'

As she left the Town Hall, she turned and faced the sea. So far and yet so near! They could stand on Calais beach on a clear day and see the silhouette of Dover Castle emerging out of the mist. No wonder the German troops arriving in Calais had asked where the 'canal' was!

How worried her parents and Rikkie her sister must be, she mused. Nellie, her mother, hadn't been too well lately, but nevertheless had invited Tom, Nell and the girls to come and stay with them in Birmingham until 'it all blew over'. They should have taken up the offer, she thought, bitterly.

And there she was being sent heaven knows where. Still, it sounded, from what she had been told, that they might be rejoining Tom. Maybe they would all land up together in the same internment camp and that wouldn't be so bad after all. At least they'd be together.

She went home and packed a bag for each of the girls to carry containing clothes, an extra pair of shoes, a toilet bag and a towel. She then rolled up a small blanket for each of them, like a long sausage, so the girls could wear it across their backs, strapped at the front. They just didn't know where they would sleep. She herself would carry a small suitcase and a bag, her fur coat doubling as a blanket.

While she was packing, one of Tom's workmen turned up. He touched his forelock. 'Beg pardon, Madame Tom, I've been sent for Monsieur Tom's car. All the English foremen's cars are going to be walled up, so the Boche won't get their hands on them.'

And so they were. A wall was built around the cars and they didn't see the light of day again until the end of the war.

The next morning, at ten o'clock sharp, Nell and the girls climbed aboard a German army lorry with wooden slatted seats down each side. There were other women and children, mostly French wives of British men. Nell was to meet very few other English women on her travels.

The lorry stopped for the night at a place called Les Attaques. A tall soldier served a German army issue meal from a large drum, and Jeanne went up for seconds. The German laughed and shook his head as he served her. He couldn't believe that anyone could actually like the stuff.

They were escorted in a group across the road to the school lavatories. The French women called out bawdy suggestions concerning the armed guard's mother, his sisters, and his own lack of manhood. The young soldier looked the other way, embarrassed. He had no doubt what was being said and you could see his point of view. He hadn't joined the mighty German army to play nursemaid to a lot of women and children.

The three girls joined two young men throwing stones at a plum tree in the vicarage garden next door, hoping the fruit would fall their way, until the village priest came out of his back door and told them off. They all retreated back inside, giggling. These two young men landed in the men's internment camp a little later and were able to tell Tom that his family was also on the move.

They arrived at Lille the next day. Marching through the street they were filmed by a German army news team on a lorry, Jeanne at the front, grinning up at the camera.

They were taken in the afternoon to Caserne Negrier, an army barracks, only to be told that the men had left just hours before; moved on for an unknown destination.

They lined up and were handed each a hunk of bread and a mug of coffee by a Catholic Youth group. Jeanne must have been hungry for she remembered the meal long afterwards.

The children spread out to familiarise themselves with their new surroundings. Some came running up. 'There's a prisoner, we've found a prisoner!' They all ran over in a group. The young man was imprisoned in a cellar, looking out of the barred window at ground level. He stared dolefully at the children and the children stared at him. Not a word was spoken.

In the early evening they were on their way again.

They arrived at Marc-en-Bareuil on the outskirts of Lille, a Catholic Priests' training college that had been requisitioned as a 'sorting-out' concentration camp for anyone who wasn't French. Whole circuses from Eastern Europe, gypsies, travellers returning from holiday, cabaret turns, foreigners who had lived in France for years, they all landed up at the College des Pretres de Marc-en-Bareuil.

Nell and the girls were in the English wing of the college, along with the families from Calais and others who had joined them from nearby towns. They were to be there for six weeks.

The German guards there weren't fighting men, but

rather those too old or sick to be at the front and were longing to go home. The Commandant, friendly and rotund, looked more suited to running a pub than a concentration camp. He was immediately nicknamed Gros-plein-de-soupe (Fatty-full-of-soup) by the inmates.

Camp life was very boring. Time lay heavy on everyone's hands and some of the children got up to mischief. A Romanian circus boy pulled a knife out in an argument with an English boy and scandalised the residents of the English wing.

They would file into the refectory at meal times. A massive hairless man with huge hands stood by the door, guillotining the bread. Jeanne was very frightened of him and would hurry past him. They ate unappetising ersatz (substitute) German food and drank lime tea or water. The diet was monotonous to the extreme.

The priests and nuns were still living at the college, sometimes seen emerging from doors marked 'private'. They didn't speak but welcomed the internees to Mass. For the first time Jeanne attended a Catholic service. It gave her something to do. She found it so beautiful: the pale blue ceiling of the small chapel studded with silver stars; the kind faces of the painted statues; the lovely music. It was a haven of peace to a homeless girl.

After a month, they were allowed a trip into Lille – under armed guard of course. The group of half-a-dozen or so women and children were as chattering and excited as giggly girls going to their first dance. They ate in a soup kitchen. Lovely homemade soup and dry bread to dip in it was such a change from the boring camp food. Grey figures slid into the soup kitchen, ate silently, and slid out again, wordlessly. Were they on the run? Were they spies? One didn't ask too many questions in occupied France.

After six weeks, an empty house was opened up for the family locally and, soon after, Nell enrolled the girls at the nearest school, a Convent school. Although she didn't know what the future held, she felt that it was important that the girls carry on with their education. It was what Tom would have wished.

Irene reported back after a week there. 'We have sewing every afternoon. We sit in a circle and while we sew we have to take it in turns to say the rosary. The small beads are equal to a Hail Mary, and every tenth bead is a larger one, and that's the Lord's Prayer. And all that time Sister Genevieve sits at the head of the circle, perched on a high stool, like an overstuffed penguin!' Irene had a way with words. She went on, 'Only the smallest, most minute stitches will do. If she's not satisfied, Sister G. makes us unpick it and start all over again! And I try so hard, I keep pricking myself. Look!' She showed them her handiwork: a handkerchief hem with the smallest, neatest stitches they had ever seen, and, by each stitch, a single bloodstain, such was her effort.

After a month, the owners of the house returned and so they were moved again to another house nearby.

The next family would not be back in a hurry. They

were English and had fled to England at the outbreak of war, leaving everything behind. There they were, smiling a welcome out of the photo frames in the sitting room: Mr and Mrs Cook and their two daughters. Outside the house a beautiful Alsatian dog stood guard but Nell found it impossible to feed it and had to give it away.

Anyone who has lived through the winter of 1941 will tell you it was one of the coldest on record; the snow and ice seemed to last for months. But Nell and the girls were safe and cosy with English books to read, and the Cook girls' toys to play with. As Christmas approached, Marie found a box marked 'Crib' in the attic. She brought it down and set it up in the sitting room, which glowed in the candlelight. It brought a little of the magic of Christmas to them.

Irene had found a book of English Christmas carols and the girls sang them for Nell. Jeanne just about managed to twist her French vowel sounds around the difficult English words.

Around this time, Irene, on her way to school, rescued a kitten being stoned by a gang of boys. She clutched the shivering bundle to her chest and pleaded with Nell to be allowed to keep it. The little kitten gave them hours of fun. Nell called it Tom because he was so affectionate. Tom would climb on her shoulder and pinch food from her mouth!

Then, as spring came, with no warning, they were on the move again for an unknown destination. As Jeanne left the convent school for the last time, she burst into tears.

It wasn't that she had been particularly happy or unhappy there, she was just tired of being uprooted, she wanted to know that she belonged somewhere. Sister Agnes, Jeanne's form teacher, turned to two girls who were being kept behind for detention, and said spitefully, 'Look, she's crying, she's sorry to leave us, and she's done nothing. It's you, you bad girls, who should be sent away!'

5. Hardship Days

Cambrai at first sight was a sad, grey town full of sad, grey people.

Twenty-five years earlier, the town had been at the forefront of First World War fighting, the scene of the first full-scale tank battle in history. The small town had never fully recovered. Traces of the heavy fighting could still be seen on the pitted houses.

Nell and the girls were taken down an old, unkempt street. They stopped in front of a tall forbidding house and the front door was opened. The owners had fled and their home was now the ground floor of this house.

There were two rooms. The living room had a large, old-fashioned dining table, a pot-bellied stove and a connecting double door through to another room. In better days this would have been the dining room, but it now housed two double beds and a washstand. The kitchen was at the end of a long, cheerless corridor. Jeanne found that if she ran down the whole length of the hall with her palm held outwards against the wall, her hand was all shiny by the time she reached the end. A glass door led into the kitchen, a damp, cold, gloomy semi-basement, going through to a scullery as ancient as could be, with old pot sinks and an antique gas stove. Nell was to cook and wash in these conditions for the next three-and-a-half years. How she must have longed for her state-of-the-art thirties kitchen with its modern gadgets and for Clothilde, her maid back in Calais.

Through the glass door there was another door through to a small courtyard with the lavatory in the corner. This was not a modern water closet, but an old-fashioned type with a lever, which opened a lid in the bottom of the pan. It was stinking in the summer and freezing cold in the winter. A big water jug had to be refilled constantly from the kitchen tap for flushing. In winter, the ice had to be broken before pouring. On a nail was a supply of newspaper squares acting as loo paper.

From the small, square yard there were a few steps up into the garden, which was sunless and enclosed by high walls on which tiny grapes never ripened.

Two Frenchwomen lived upstairs in the house: Englishmen's wives. Jannie had the front room and Raymonde the back one. They had the bathroom of the house but no kitchen and cooked in their rooms.

Up another set of stairs was a large, empty attic including two rooms, the maids' bedrooms no doubt. There was a powerful, closed-in, dusty, fusty, old-ladyish sort of smell about the place. Irene and Jeanne found a suitcase full of old clothes. Irene was very good at making up plays and dances, and she and Jeanne spent hours in the attic playing games of make-believe.

If they looked out of the windows at the front of the attic, they could see right over the high walls of the convent opposite into a lovely garden full of trees. Occasionally they even saw the nuns walking sedately along the paths.

Apart from the attic and the forlorn garden, there was very little to do and very little space to do it in.

It was around this time that Nell heard that her mother had died back in January two months before — just after her mother had heard that Nell and the girls were safe. The only means of communication was through Tom. Gramp and Rikkie wrote the sad news to him, and he in turn wrote to Nell. Nell was only allowed a twenty-five-word message once every six months through the kind auspices of the Swiss Red Cross. Tom, on the other hand, was allowed two letters and two postcards to France and one letter and two postcards to England a month. So it fell to Tom to write and tell Nell that her beloved mother's funeral had been and gone and she had not known anything about it. It was extremely hard for Nell. These turned out to be the hardest times for her and she hardly had time to mourn.

Settling in, Nell found she was required to sign on at the *Kommandantur* once a month, and that she was not allowed to travel anywhere without a special permit. Otherwise they were free to lead a normal life.

After she had got rid of the fleas from the house, her next priority was to find schools for the girls. Marie, aged fourteen-and-a-half, had been a serious, straight-haired, bespectacled child. She was enrolled at the co-ed technical college on a business course and within a short space of time turned into a beautiful teenager, popular with everyone and always full of fun.

Nell next applied to the College Fenelon for Girls hoping to get both Irene and Jeanne accepted. They had attended the girls' college in Calais, and it seemed the obvious choice for them.

Mademoiselle Provino, the headmistress, sat at her desk and considered. In her unrelieved black dress with a white ruff at the throat, a tight chignon and a pince-nez on the end of her nose, she was straight out of a Victorian novel. She had quick, pert movements, and nine-year-old Jeanne, squirming uncomfortably in her chair, likened her to a farmyard bird – a bantam hen, perhaps, or a guinea fowl.

Mademoiselle Provino and Nell discussed Irene's education at length. Irene, was thirteen and bore the burden of being the clever one of the family. She was prepared to work and Mademoiselle Provino was pleased; she liked studious 'gels'.

She next turned her acid smile towards Jeanne, fixing her with her small bird's piercing eyes, ready to peck at a choice morsel. 'And this is Number Three, is it?'

Jeanne wished she were a thousand miles away. She

wasn't prepared to work. There were far more interesting things to do.

From that day on Jeanne was referred to as 'Number Three' by Mademoiselle Provino, and was to be a constant thorn in the headmistress's side.

The Germans always requisitioned the best buildings of a town for their own use. The fine hotel on the main square, the casino, the newest and best cinema; all these had been taken over in Cambrai and the French population had to make do with what was left over. The beautiful, newly-built College Fenelon was now a hospital for sick and wounded German soldiers.

The college girls were cramped and squashed into an entirely unsuitable building on the other side of the town. It was behind an unimposing facade, through a carriage entrance into a courtyard. This was the college playground. There were no sports fields, no grounds, just a yard for break and lunchtime. It was the same inside the building. The girls were hopelessly overcrowded, the rooms quite inadequate as classrooms.

Jeanne's class was taught by an old lady, far too old to be dealing with a pack of mischievous nine-year-olds. The girls teased her mercilessly and made her life a misery. She was given to repeating herself and the girls kept a score of every '*alors*' and '*eh bien*' she uttered during the lesson.

They would chew a piece of paper until it was pulp, draw a paper parachutist, cut it out and attach it with a thread to the papier maché and flick it up to the ceiling with a ruler. There it would dangle for the next month or so, until it dried out, to the great annoyance of Mademoiselle. At times, the high ceiling was studded with a whole army of parachutists, all waiting patiently for their day to come when they would drop on a pupil's head. When that happened, the whole class erupted and pandemonium ruled.

In the winter everyone wore their coats in class. At the start of the lesson, the girls argued and jostled and the lucky ones ended up sitting by the inadequate pot-bellied stove at the back of the classroom. It was replenished at regular intervals during the lesson by the teacher.

When Jeanne had her turn by the stove, she would put her apple on top of it at the start of the lesson. If the teacher hadn't seen it and told her to remove it, she had a half-cooked apple by break time, warm and delicious.

At break they were made to queue up for two casein biscuits each, which the government provided as a protein replacement. Protein was lacking in the children's diet, milk being in such short supply. The pupils got thoroughly sick of them and fed them to the caretaker's dog, who finished up a fat, matted teddy bear – the best fed dog in occupied France!

Meanwhile, what of Tom?

When the British men had left Caserne Negrier, in Lille, they were taken to the infamous Loos prison nearby and put in solitary confinement. Every now and then, sitting in his cell, Tom heard someone being marched out to the courtyard and shot. He suffered torments, wondering when his turn would come.

'They can't shoot me,' he reasoned. 'I haven't done anything wrong, I'm a civilian, a family man.' But lying sleepless at night, doubts and fears would overcome him, making him question the sanity of his captors, imagining an odd, trigger-happy gunman.

'And Nell and the girls. What's happened to them? Where, oh where are they? Are they all right?' Poor Tom, confined to his solitary cell, wondered what their fate would be.

After a few days, the men were moved to Belgium: first to Liege prison, then on to the impregnable Huy prison fortress. More men joined them, day by day.

Whenever he was allowed to write a letter, he wrote to Nell in Calais, to the neighbours, to his firm – anyone he could think of, hoping for news by some means or other. He was not to hear from Nell for fourteen weeks.

Tom never spoke much of his incarceration in Huy afterwards. It was his worst experience. When they left after a few weeks, he barely had the strength to carry his cases across the yard.

A total of 850 men were put in cattle trucks for an unknown destination and, after an unspeakable journey of three days and nights without food, arrived at Tost, near Gleiwitz on the Polish border (now Toszak in Poland). There, a redundant lunatic asylum, 'cleansed' of its occupants by the Nazi system, was opened up and made into an internment camp for 1,300 British civilians. For Tom and his friends from Calais, this period was to be a long saga of deprivation, humiliation and boredom. To quote Tom in one of his letters, 'Wife, family, house, job, car, all "Gone with the Wind".'

Nell too was having a hard time. Being a Britisher in wartime France, her assets were frozen and she wasn't allowed to withdraw money from her bank account. First she had to apply for charity. She also had to manage on a small French government prisoner-of-war allowance, and a similar one from Courtaulds in Calais. It didn't amount to much and was precious little when you had to feed three hungry, growing girls. She found it extremely difficult to make ends meet. At times she took in washing and taught English.

Anything could be had on the black market, of course. It was a topsy-turvy world: the butcher sold coal; the hat shop, eggs; the sweet shop, meat; but all at an inflated price that Nell couldn't afford. Also there was little or no gas, and electricity was restricted too. Sunday was the only day when there was enough gas to boil up the washing. It was not unusual to be entirely without salt, soap, sugar, potatoes, coal or eggs, all at the same time, and Nell never saw any tinned goods of any kind. Sausages and chips were a distant memory! The monthly coffee issue consisted of a few coffee beans at the top of a large bag, which were scooped up and kept for a special occasion, then a layer of chicory. The rest was roasted grains, barley perhaps. It was awful, but did make a hot drink of sorts. The bread was dark brown, soggy, unappetising and better eaten stale, usually without precious butter or margarine. They often spread it with mashed potato or stewed apple. Jam was awful. Nell suspected it was flavoured swede. She always crossed a new loaf of bread with the knife before cutting it; an old superstition that meant they would never go without bread.

Often the main meal consisted of black-market potatoes with swede one day, carrots the next – boiled of course; there was not a scrap of extra fat to be had.

Being under thirteen, Jeanne was the only one of them eligible for a milk ration, a quarter of a litre every two days, which Nell used in their ration coffee to make it more palatable. On the other hand, Nell, Marie and Irene had a wine ration, and Jeanne shared it with them.

'Drink it. It's full of iron,' Nell would say.

Jeanne also got a monthly bar of inferior chocolate, which was ceremoniously cut into four sections and distributed among them.

No food was imported into occupied France. Anything the least bit luxurious such as tomatoes, olive oil and good wine, found its way to Germany. Winter was especially hard: only root vegetables, potatoes, cabbage or apples, the most basic of foods, were available.

People who were lucky enough to have relatives or

friends who lived in the country would strap a basket on their bike and cycle out to collect fresh eggs, butter and even occasionally a chicken. Nell had no such luck. Had she stayed in Calais where she had many friends, she would have been able to take advantage of such connections. But here in Cambrai, she knew no one.

She tried growing her own vegetables in the back garden, but the soil was poor, and her self-esteem would not allow her to follow the coalman's horse and cart with a bucket and shovel to pick up the steaming horse droppings, which might have improved it. She kept rabbits in a lean-to at the end of the garden, and made it plain to Jeanne from the outset that these were not pets, but for eating.

On the appointed day, she and Jeanne selected one of the rabbits. They felt each one in turn and decided which one was most ready for the pot. The chosen one was pulled out of the hutch, struggling and fighting. Nell gave it a 'karate chop' on the back of the neck. It fought a little then went limp. The dead rabbit was hung up on the lean-to wall by its back legs. Like all good housewives of the time, Nell knew how to skin a rabbit. She told Jeanne as she worked, 'It's easier to skin it while it's still warm. See, it just comes off like a pair of pyjamas!' And so it did. Nell pulled and tugged at the pelt and it came away easily, inside out, all in one go. She then cut a slit right down the rabbit's abdomen, plunged her hand into the cavity, and pulled out the entrails. Jeanne, holding a bowl underneath, watched in fascinated horror as the disgusting, steaming, smelly mess spilled into it. Nell retrieved the heart and liver, saying they were the best bits and, arms bloody to the elbows, tidied up the extremities with a sharp knife, and cut the rabbit's head off, setting it aside for tomorrow's soup. The rabbit was ready for the pot.

She then said, 'Go and tell Marie I've been able to get the skin off all in one go. She wants to stretch it and see if she can back her new mittens with the fur.' Nothing was ever wasted.

Marie's experiment was not a success. Although she did back the mittens, within a week or so, the lovely pale grey fur came away in handfuls and the mittens were ruined.

Nell was forever chasing food. She spent long hours queueing for meat, vegetables and bread. She would be down at the Boucherie Chevaline at 5.30am, joining the queue for a piece of cheap horsemeat. She couldn't afford to be fussy: this was wartime. Tom was complaining how few letters he received, always begging for more news. But Nell didn't want to confide in him just how difficult things were. After all, he was locked up and shouldn't be worried, and anyway she had very little time to write letters.

In pre-war days Nell had been, to put it kindly, voluptuous. She had matched Tom's appetite for the good life and had a lot of weight to lose. However, Marie hadn't and was getting painfully thin. They tried to make light of it, laughing and quoting their own private joke to each other, 'Five francs left till the end of the month!'

Then she had a stroke of luck.

She and the girls had been kindly received by the only Protestant church in Cambrai and, hearing of their plight, the small congregation offered to pay for Irene and Jeanne's school dinners. This was wonderful news for Nell. She now knew that two of her girls would get a square meal every school day. She accepted gratefully.

After some time a letter came from their Calais neighbour, May Youll. Her husband Sandy was in camp with Tom. May was held in a nearby women's internment camp in northern France. She enclosed a photo of herself, looking fit and well, she said, because of the Red Cross parcels.

This was news to Nell. It was the first she'd heard of Red Cross parcels. She was sure she too must qualify and it would make all the difference to them.

After making some enquiries, she wrote to the large internment camp centre at Vittel, claiming her right to Red Cross parcels. The answer came: 'Parcels are exclusively for internees, people behind barbed wire. Sorry, but you do not qualify.'

She then approached the German authorities, begging that she and the girls be interned. Even if they were locked up, she reasoned, at least they would get enough to eat. The Germans were just as adamant. 'Families do not qualify for internment camp. Families stay free, signing on monthly. The children must continue with their schooling.' So she was back where she started: 'Five francs left till the end of the month!'

Some time later, trying every avenue that might be

open to her, she heard of a possible loan through neutral Switzerland. She applied and, to her great delight and relief, they were allocated a small monthly sum of money, just enough to help them out.

From that day on, she and Marie had enough to eat. They ate at a cheap restaurant nearby where there were two systems of payment. You either paid the lower price, in which case ration tickets were handed over for meat, bread and butter, or you paid the higher, black market, price. Nell chose the higher price, saving the precious ration tickets for evenings and weekends when the family was together. The system worked well, though Nell swore that the 'Rabbit Chasseur' they enjoyed at the restaurant regularly, was in fact Cat Chasseur!

1941 — 1944

6. Settling in Days

Jeanne was settling into her new life. It really didn't look as if they were going to be moved again this time.

The main square in Cambrai, the Grand Place, was where the imposing town hall stood. Effigies of the town's heroes, Martin and Martine, stood either side of the clock tower, and every hour a carillon rang out playing their tune. The *Kommandantur* covered in flags and swastikas stood at one end of the square and the casino at the other.

Most of her school friends were Catholic, and thought she was strange attending the tiny Protestant church. She enjoyed it so much, especially the singing. She loved singing. The minister, Pere Lacheret, became a surrogate father to the family, always ready with comfort and advice. He had been a missionary in French New Caledonia in the Pacific, and had returned home to France with his wife and four children at the outbreak of war. He was a fine, handsome man with a long black beard and flashing eyes.

He stuttered, except when he gave a sermon. Then he never stuttered at all. Jeanne adored him.

The church was also used by many of the German soldiers who were Lutheran Protestants. They filed out after their Sunday service, having prayed to God for victory. The French and German ministers exchanged courteous greetings then the French congregation filed in, sat down, and prayed to God for victory, so that the Germans might all go home and leave them to live in peace!

At Christmas time, the Germans put a huge Christmas tree by the altar and decorated it with sparkling cotton. Jeanne thought she had never seen anything so lovely. She sat with her friends and sang carols to her heart's content.

After church, if they could afford it, Nell and the girls picked up a cake or tart from the patisserie, then walked on to the one remaining cinema not requisitioned by the Germans to book for the evening's performance. They saw every film that was ever shown at the little picture house; it was the week's treat and they never missed it. This was long before the days of television and the internet. It was their only entertainment.

Before the main film, they were treated to German newsreels showing how well their boys were doing on the Russian or North African fronts. They saw RAF planes shot down by the valiant airmen of the Luftwaffe, young fresh-faced Germans coping admirably in all adversity. Nell had to be almost held down in her seat, she would get so angry. Footage of Hitler and Mussolini meeting somewhere or other was also shown; the same pompous march by Sibelius was always played at such times.

Then came the main film, the one they had come to see. They saw dubbed German films: costume extravaganzas about the Strauss family ad nauseam; German-made musicals with stars such as Zara Leander; and tear-jerkers – stories of German soldiers leaving for the front and sweethearts waiting for their return. They also saw low budget French films made on a shoestring where beautiful ladies sang to incredibly handsome men in fantasy lands where there were no wars and the sun always shone. They even saw a colour film from Czechoslovakia. Very garish, but a novelty nevertheless. It was all such a treat.

Jeanne lapped it all up. For her, this was real life and where she wanted to be. She truly wished that she could step right through the screen and be part of that other world. She had made up her mind: she was going to be a film star.

On Saturdays, she met her friends at the market on the main square. She never had any money to spend but liked to play the What-would-I-buy-if-I had-ten-francs? game, going from stall to stall, taking her time and choosing carefully. She particularly liked books about film stars: their private lives, their loves, their homes. Yes, that is what she would buy if she had ten francs, a film star book full of colour photos. A book about Charles Trenet, or Danielle Darrieux, or Fernandel perhaps? She liked Fernandel; he was funny.

In the centre of the market, they watched the 'Song Man'

for hours. He sang hits from the latest films, acting them out with lewd gestures and making his audience laugh. When he had finished the people in the crowd bought his song sheets. Jeanne and Irene knew the words to all the songs from the films and would sing and dance to them in the garden or the attic when they got home. Jeanne never had enough money for the song sheets but, when she could, she bought a shiny black-and-white postcard-sized photo of one of the film stars. She amassed a sizeable collection, twenty or twenty-five of them. The men were so handsome, cigarette held aloft in an elegant hand, and the aloof ladies wore long slinky dresses covered in sequins or beads and had shining lips and languorous eyes averted from the camera. Jeanne treasured her photos. She kept them in a shoebox under the bed and got them out frequently to look at.

One Saturday while out on her own, she bumped into Madeleine, one of her school friends, who was out with her parents. She was arm-in-arm with a young man who was introduced as her fiancé. Jeanne was horrified: Madeleine was twelve years old – Jeanne's age – yet the young man had been chosen as a suitor by her parents. Jeanne ran home in a panic and told Nell what had happened. She didn't want to get married yet! 'Please, please, don't let me be married yet!' Nell laughed and said it was very unlikely and told her to go away and finish her homework.

Sometimes a squad of German soldiers marched down the middle of the street returning from the baths, the conquering heroes. Stripped to the waist, with towels round their necks, they marched and sang as they marched in perfect unison. It went something like:

'*I-ye, i-yo,*
I-ye, i-yo.'

French urchins followed, singing from the pavement and ready to dart down the nearest side street should they be chased.

'*Du riz au lait*
Pour les Anglais.
Du riz a l'eau
Pour les salauds!'

Which translates roughly as:

'Rice with milk
For the English.
Rice with water
For the bastards!'

In the summer, the youth of Cambrai flocked to the swimming pool. It was their social centre and meeting place. Within these walls they could run about and splash and misbehave to their heart's content, forgetting the repression outside. Jeanne and her friends spent many happy hours there.

It was on a calm Sunday morning, when there weren't many people about, that Jeanne launched herself into the deep pool, four metres deep. She had spent a long time practising breaststroke in the shallow pool, one foot on the bottom, and now felt ready to literally take the plunge.

She heard Marie scream, 'Jeanne! My sister! She can't swim!' But Jeanne carried on swimming. One of Marie's admirers obligingly dived in to the rescue, wanting to prove himself and be a hero in Marie's eyes. He found that Jeanne was coping perfectly well and so swam by her side, encouraging her until she reached the other end where Marie was waiting to tell her off, more out of relief than anger. But Jeanne was happy. She could now call herself a swimmer.

Coming home from school one day with Nicole, they came across a new poster down a side street. The authorities were always putting up posters telling the population how well off they were or for certain named men to give themselves up. This was a really lurid one, showing Allied planes flying over Joan of Arc on her burning pyre, houses blazing in the background, all in deepest red, yellow and black. Underneath was written, THE ASSASSINS HAVE RETURNED TO THE SCENE OF THEIR CRIME. Nicole and Jeanne were offended by this and felt that something must be done. People were often trying to tear down these posters. It made you feel a bit better if you were successful. Searching their school bags, one found a nail file, the other a metal ruler, and they set to work scraping at it and trying to remove it, keeping an eye out in case someone saw them. The glue proved far too strong and they had to reluctantly leave it to be admired or hated, depending on one's point of view.

At this time, Marie longed for her piano back in Calais. The trouble was that she had begun to prove that she was really talented and would have had a really successful future in front of her but Nell couldn't afford expensive piano lessons. She was always on the look-out for a piano when visiting friends and, upon finding one, would exclaim, 'Oh, a piano!' She was delighted when given permission to play and was eventually allowed to practise regularly at a friend's house. Her musical hero was Frederick Chopin and she took great delight in schooling her long, slim fingers in trying to play his *Fantaisie Impromptu*, her favourite. She was unable to fulfil her ultimate ambition though.

Dressing the girls was a nightmare for Nell. Apart from the shortage of money, there were the dreaded clothing coupons. Each time a new allocation was made, Nell had to do a balancing act to decide which item of clothing was most needed. If she put the coupons towards a new pair of shoes for Irene, providing she could afford it, of course, she couldn't buy warm winter underwear for Jeanne; and a new coat for one of them would take the whole allocation for all the family. It was unthinkable for Nell to buy anything on the expensive black market, so very few new clothes came their way.

Marie became extremely adept at making do. From the age of fifteen she was always smartly dressed in the latest fashion. Her long, delicate, fingers were constantly busy, sewing a blouse maybe and adding a bit of lace – begged, borrowed or recycled – on the cuffs and at the neckline.

Or she would take an old skirt apart and, lo and behold, an embroidered waistcoat would appear. She also became an expert knitter. Buying knitting wool would have meant using some of the already-spoken-for clothing coupons, so if she wanted a new jumper she had to unpick one or combine two old ones to get enough wool to knit a new one. First, she carefully unpicked the seams, revealing the back, the front and two sleeves, then she started unravelling the back. The wool ran free but crinkly, and it was at this stage that she had to get hold of a volunteer. 'Jca-a-nne . . .!'

Jeanne had her elbow on the sideboard and ear glued to the radio. 'What?'

Marie said sweetly, 'Come and give me a hand, please. I need some help.'

Jeanne said crossly, 'Can't, I'm busy.'

'If you're listening to the radio, we'll move over closer. I only need you to hold your hands up while I wind the wool.'

Jeanne snapped, 'Yes, yes, I know what you want me for.'

Irene, from the depths of the only armchair with her nose in a book, said, 'Shut up, you two. I've got to learn this speech for French Lit by tomorrow. It's two pages long!'

Marie and Jeanne quoted in unison, '*Albe, Mon cher pays, Mon premier amour . . .*' In the confined space, they knew the speech as well as Irene did.

Marie whispered conspiratorially, 'If you help me, I'll let you come and sit with us at the pool tomorrow.'

Now, *that* was really something. Sitting with Marie and

her friends, who were always surrounded by hordes of boys, with all the banter, the mock fights and the throwings in. How envious Nicole and Jeanne's other friends would be when they saw her with Marie's friends. Jeanne agreed grudgingly. 'Oh, all right then.' She'd fallen for it again. It was more than likely that tomorrow, when Jeanne approached Marie and her friends sitting by the pool, Marie would have completely forgotten her promise and send Jeanne packing. She fell for it every time.

Jeanne now sat opposite Marie with her hands up in front of her nose, a foot apart, while Marie wound the unpicked wool around Jeanne's hands into skeins. Jeanne had to sit like this for hours until the whole jumper was unwound, and she got the sharp end of Marie's tongue if her hands started to droop.

Once the unwinding process was complete and the skeins made up, they were washed carefully and threaded through a broom handle, which was then rested between two chairs and left to drip overnight in a bowl. When dry, the wool was nice and straight and the kinks gone. Marie now needed a volunteer again and, yes, you've guessed it, Jeanne was enlisted. The skein was again put on Jeanne's outstretched hands and the whole process was repeated in reverse, only this time the wool was wound into balls ready for knitting. Using this method, the wool was recycled several times over, reappearing as a two-tone jumper or a scarf and glove set or a pair of thick winter socks until it was finally too old and matted to be of further use. Marie could also knit gloves and socks on four needles, turn heels and do the most complicated Fair Isle patterns. Nothing was too much of a challenge for her.

Having a head full of lice was a social stigma. Children with lice were shunned.

Jeanne had lice. There was no doubt about it. She scratched and scratched, the irritation driving her mad. Nell lathered her head with 'Marie-Rose', a pretty name for a disgusting concoction. What's more, it didn't do any good; it didn't work at all.

Jeanne panicked. Her thoughts went back to the first day at the convent school at Marc-en-Bareuil. She had asked her classroom neighbour why there was a boy in the class. The girl had tittered and answered that this was not a boy, but a lice-ridden girl and, lice being contagious, her head had been shaved.

Jeanne turned tearfully to Nell. 'They won't shave my head, Mummy, will they?'

'Well Jeannot, I don't know if they'd do it here. But you've got to be a very sensible girl and not scratch when you're at school. It wouldn't do to draw attention to yourself. I'm going to cut your hair short, as short as I dare, and I'm going to cut your finger nails very short too, then you'll have nothing to scratch with, will you?'

Since the 'Marie-Rose' didn't work, there was only one alternative.

Every evening, after they had eaten and the table had

been cleared, Jeanne sat head bent over a white sheet of paper in front of her on the table and scraped a fine-tooth comb over her scalp over and over again. The lice fell on the paper and, as they ran in all directions, she squashed the nasty things flat with her thumbnail. Then she tapped the edge of the comb on the edge of the table, and the eggs and nits, being the discarded shells of hatched eggs, fell onto the paper. This performance was repeated each evening, and after about a fortnight or so there were no more lice. The scare was over.

In these difficult days, Jeanne was a highly-strung, nervy child and an anxious Nell took her to see the local doctor, an elderly gentleman long past retirement age but the only doctor available in the district. Younger men were prisoners of war or forcibly working for the Germans, or exiled abroad waiting for better days.

The old doctor gave Jeanne a thorough examination and declared, 'There's nothing wrong with the child. Try not to excite her too much . . . no coffee, tea or wine . . . and give her good food . . . thick soup . . . stews . . .'

Nell came out of the surgery, snorting with anger. 'No coffee, tea or wine, indeed! Where would I find such luxuries? Chance would be a fine thing! Stews and thick soups? Silly old fool . . . and as for not exciting you too much . . . what with the threat of bombs and worse . . . silly old fool . . .'

When Jeanne had conjunctivitis, her eyes were glued together when she woke up in the mornings. She had to prise them open between her thumb and forefinger, first one, then the other. Nell wasn't keen to take Jeanne to the expensive old doctor again and so, morning and evening, she bathed her infected eyes with warm water, to which a little salt had been added. The infection took a long time to go, but it cleared eventually.

But worse was to come.

Many schoolchildren caught impetigo in occupied France, probably due to the poor diet, though it was also attributed to a surfeit of casein biscuits. Impetigo was awful. It could strike at any time without warning and come up in nasty looking scabs. Jeanne had it on her chin and upper lip; Irene, poor girl, on her scalp. Since it was thought at the time to be highly infectious, the affected children had to attend a clinic on the outskirts of town. Irene and Jeanne would walk down together from school and there they were subjected to a form of treatment that was basic, to say the least.

The awful scabs were removed with tweezers and the infected parts dabbed with stinging ether. Jeanne yelled, screamed and kicked – it was so painful. Then gentian violet was applied to the open wounds, and she was sent home with a purple chin and upper lip for all to see.

Finding Irene's infection difficult to deal with, her hair being in the way, the only possible course was taken: they shaved her hair off.

Then they carried out the same treatment as they did on Jeanne, and sent Irene home hairless, her head covered in purple dye. Imagine a fourteen-year-old girl with a purple head and no hair. She wore a turban, factory-girl style, and consequently was known throughout the town as '*l'Americaine*'. When she was cured, her hair grew again, fine and brown, prettier than before. But the mental and emotional scars remained long after the hair had grown back.

7. Jean, and an Awful Evening

Jean was in love. He adored Marie; he worshipped the ground she walked on.

He lived just down the road with his parents in a large house with a beautiful garden, but he would spend hours at Nell's, sprawled in the only armchair regaling them with amazing stories, tall stories, preposterous anecdotes. He was always looking to Marie for approval, hoping for a sign. But she only saw him as a brother, a good friend. She was the older woman. He was sixteen; she was seventeen.

Jean was a hothead. The great sorrow of his life, apart from his unrequited love for Marie, was that he could not take part in the war. He knew it would all be over by the time he was old enough to fight and he was just dying to have a go. But he could still find many small ways to annoy the Germans, and got up to all sorts of tricks just to get rid of his frustration.

Late at night, Nell would hear an urgent knock on the front door.

'Open up, open up . . .'

Standing behind the door, she would say fearfully, 'Who's that?'

'It's me! Jean. Open up, quick, quick . . .'

She would unlock and open the door and Jean would thrust a stolen pair of German army boots into her hands, or a can of petrol off an army lorry.

'Here,' he would say, breathless. 'Look after this for me. I'll be back later.'

'Oh no, Jean! Not at this house! Not here of all places.'

Jean would simply look over his shoulder before disappearing into the night. 'I'll see you later!' He'd done his daily bit for the war effort.

One afternoon, Jean and Marie returned from an outing, eyes sparkling. They were laughing and had a tale to tell. They had gone out in Jean's father's car to the nearby airfield and had parked by the fence. There, arms round each other pretending to kiss, they had counted the German machine-gun emplacements. Jean would report his findings to the underground movement later and feel useful in his small way.

Nell was furious. She turned on Marie. 'Don't you ever, ever do anything like that again! You know very well your father's in German hands, and should you ever get into trouble, there could be reprisals against him.'

Nell had been approached time and time again by the Resistance. With her knowledge of English, she could have been very useful to them. But she felt strongly that she had been given a job to do, and that was to get her family through this wretched war unharmed and she refused to get involved. She also suspected at times that she didn't know whether people were on her side or against her. Many of the French were resentful that their country had been invaded twice in twenty-five years and some were apt to blame the Allies as much as the Germans, and so Nell tried not to draw attention to herself too much.

But some were very friendly and she knew she could trust them.

One evening, Nell was visiting Monsieur and Madame Begue. Their son Roger was in Marie's class and they were very happy to invite her over for a chat. Nell sensed there was an atmosphere in the Begue's kitchen that night, a feeling of excitement that Nell could not fathom out at all. They talked of this and that and, as she left, she still felt puzzled; it had been a very odd evening indeed.

When Nell bumped into Madame Begue the following week, all was made clear. Nell had been sitting with her back to an R.A.F. airman sitting in the next room, waiting to be rescued! Madame Begue continued, 'We know you don't want to get involved with the Resistance and we respect your wishes.' But Nell was slightly disappointed. She would have loved to have had a chat with one of 'Our boys'.

One Sunday evening, returning in the blackest of blackouts from their weekly visit to the flea-pit, Marie fell and twisted her ankle. She just could not walk on it.

It was an awful end to an awful evening.

They had seen a costume drama, a real weepy. Marie-Antoinette was being prepared for her walk to the guillotine. A nasty, leering man had cut off her beautiful long hair with a sword and her weeping attendants had gently removed the lace collar from her neck so that the blade would cut cleanly.

Jeanne had been vaguely aware of movement in the cinema, of people walking heavily down the aisles. But she was much too engrossed in the film to take any real notice. The queen's walk to the scaffold, her head held erect, had her undivided attention. The film ended, the lights went up. Women were dabbing their eyes.

'Nobody move! Stay right where you are!' a voice shouted.

The cinema was full of German troops blocking every exit, their guns at the ready.

The audience panicked. Everyone was screaming. Women clung to their husbands or sons, really crying now.

'No, no!' they shouted. Some men tried to hide under the tip-up seats, others looked towards the toilets, but it was too late. The doors were already blocked by more armed guards.

Jeanne's hand sought Nell's and held on to it. They were herded towards the exit.

'*Papieren! Papieren!*' The soldiers were checking identity papers. Once this was established to their satisfaction, they let the women go, but the men were detained for further questioning. These events occurred frequently. Able-bodied Frenchmen were forcibly sent to Germany to help with the war effort, or to work on the Atlantic wall running along the west coast of France, built to repel any Allied invasion. Many carried forged identity papers that stated they were ill or disabled and unable to work.

The lobby was in pandemonium. Weeping women were wrenched from their men and told roughly to go home.

A voice called out, 'Marie! Marie!'

Marie gasped. 'My goodness, it's Paul, one of the boys from college. They've got him!'

Paul shouted, trying to make his voice heard above the commotion. 'Marie, go and tell my mother I've been arrested. Can you hear me?'

She waved and tried to smile reassuringly. Poor Paul! She wondered what would happen to him. She turned to Nell and her sisters. 'Come on, I know where he lives, it's just round the corner. His poor mother! What a shock.'

They forced their way through the crowd gathered outside the cinema and were soon at Paul's house. They knocked on the door. A first-floor window opened cautiously and a frightened voice said, 'Who is it?' People always feared a nocturnal knock on the door.

'It's me, Marie Sarginson. We've come from the cinema. Paul's been picked up.' They heard a gasp and the window closed. Within seconds, Madame Dupuis was on the doorstep in her dressing gown and they gave her as much information as they could.

When they had delivered their message, they walked on towards home, discussing the evening's events. Surely Paul, being only seventeen and still at college, would be released? Paul was indeed freed, but immediately disappeared. His mother had decided he might not be so lucky next time. He was, it was said, 'en forêt'. Working in forestry was a euphemism in wartime France for 'he's in hiding' or 'he's joined the Resistance'.

It was on the way home that Marie fell and twisted her ankle. She just could not walk on it. They stood around her in the pitch-dark blackout, the inadequate light of Nell's torch shining feebly on Marie's ankle, not quite knowing what to do next, when, incongruously, they heard someone walking down the street, cheerfully whistling Geraldo's signature tune, straight off the forbidden BBC broadcasts: *He-llo again. We're on the radi-o again . . .*

There was only one person in German-occupied Cambrai who had the audacity to do such a thing.

'Jean! Jean . . .Come here, over here!' they called.

That night, Jean got his heart's desire. He scooped Marie up in his arms and, holding her close to him, carried her home.

Much, much later, after the liberation, a man stood on their doorstep resplendent in brand-new uniform. It was Jean, the youngest brigadier in the French army!

8. Internment Days

Tom was settling in to internment camp life.

The 1,300 British internees were from all over Europe. Some had even been caught at sea, including a boatload of missionaries. Tom used to say that in the camp, the Bible was translated into whatever language you cared to mention. Seventeen languages were spoken. The only language to beat the censors at the large centre in Breslau was Welsh. In consequence, letters in Welsh were banned.

The small group of internees from Calais had been able to stay together. They were in Room 309, on the third floor of the old lunatic asylum; sixty-six men crammed in a room meant for thirty inmates. They made the best of these difficult conditions, but it wasn't easy.

Among them was P. G. Wodehouse, the humorist, picked up from his house in Le Touquet. He wrote at length about camp life in his book *The Performing Flea*, mentioning 'that rare soul Tom Sarginson' among others. Tom didn't like him very much, though. The great man treated camp life as a 'Jolly Jape', and Tom thought it nothing like a jolly jape. Tom just wanted to be back home with his wife and family. He endured the situation and hoped it wouldn't last too long.

Wodehouse described how, when a loaf of German Army issue bread was thrown onto the dinner table to be divided between nine internees, Tom took his steel rule out and measured accurately, making sure that the sloped end portions were a little deeper. Everyone watched Tom like a hawk and woe betide him should the knife have slipped!

Tom noticed early on that some men were not coping at all well with their imprisonment. In particular, a man he knew well had become a little grey-haired old man almost overnight, shuffling to and fro from his bunk looking lost. Tom resolved to keep fit in mind and body so that, whenever the war ended, he could take up his life where he had left off. He found that men who had been to boarding school or ex-servicemen like himself, coped best of all.

At various times he was a deputy Camp Captain, a Red Cross committee member, learned German, taught French, volunteered to help build a dam, took up painting and model making and passed five School Certificates (old GCSEs) including English. He wrote to Gramp and Rikkie, 'Takes one war to learn English and another to improve it. One war to introduce me to ladies and another to keep me away!'

He would also walk round the perimeter of the camp four times every evening, the equivalent of one mile, to keep himself fit.

Life was much easier for the men once the all-important

Red Cross parcels started to arrive. Gone were the days of smoking thrice-used tea leaves, and cleaning one's teeth with the ash. Bartering became the order of the day. If one bartered wisely, one had no need to go without ever again. The non-smokers were particularly favoured. The parcels always contained a tin of fifty cigarettes, and a non-smoker could hold a smoker to ransom, swapping his unwanted cigarettes for all sorts of goodies. Parcels also began arriving from friends and relatives. They had to be five pounds in weight. If a parcel didn't quite reach that weight, the Red Cross would add a pair of gloves or socks to make the weight up.

Nell's sister Elsie, known as 'Rikkie', which she preferred, worked tirelessly to send whatever she could. She also wrote to the Red Cross in Birmingham and to whomever she could to see if Nell could also receive parcels but nothing ever came of it. She made such a nuisance of herself that she became Chairman of the local Prisoner of War Society, which amused her greatly.

Tom would occasionally send coded messages. For instance if he said he was pleased to hear that Rikkie's firm was doing well, it was a way of saying that there was a radio concealed in the camp and that they could hear the BBC news. (Rikkie was personal assistant to the regional director of the BBC in Birmingham.) But when he mentioned Monsieur Salva, the Italian greengrocer back home, Nell said, 'Why has he mentioned Monsieur Salva, I hardly knew the man!'

'He's talking about the Italians and their position in the war!' Irene said. And they noticed that Tom wrote about Boris, the only Russian they knew in Calais, with the same general meaning.

Many of the men were musicians or performers who had been touring the Continent and had been caught at the outbreak of war. Through the Red Cross they were able to have costumes and musical instruments sent over, and Tom said that some of the shows he saw were every bit as good as anything he had seen on the professional stage.

Of course, with so many men cooped up for such a long time, all sorts of mischief occurred. The men had observed that their scraps of inedible food were fed to the camp pigs. But when they realised that the pigs were actually going to feed the guards and not the internees, the pigs died mysteriously. The men had chopped up used razor blades into tiny pieces and mixed them in with the scraps!

Tom was learning German and undertook his own propaganda campaign. Taking a newly arrived can of lamb's tongues, he showed it to one of the guards and said, 'Look, I've just received this tin, it holds six lamb's tongues. There are 1,300 internees in the camp, and they have all received a similar can. 1,300 times six is 7,800. That means 7,800 lambs were slaughtered so that the internees in this camp could have a can of lamb's tongues each! What chance have you of winning the war against such might?'

Tom was not alone in his sense of humour. When the Camp Commandant did his round, he was followed by a retinue of four corporals, guns slung over one shoulder. P.G. Wodehouse wrote in his memoir *The Performing Flea* that the men would say, 'Here they come, "Ginger, Rosebud, Pluto and Donald Duck" and they would roar with laughter.'

After ten months, P.G. Wodehouse received an offer by the German authorities to go and stay in a Hotel in Berlin in perfect freedom and his wife Ethel, who was held in an internment camp for women in northern France, would be free to join him. He would broadcast amusing lectures about life in internment camp to his many friends in neutral America who had been pressing for his release. This he accepted, and although there was no harm at all in the lectures, it caused consternation back in Britain. Questions were asked in Parliament and he was branded a traitor. He was never able to return home and spent the rest of his life in the United States. He was forgiven and knighted on January 1st 1975 and died a few weeks later, aged 93. There is a plaque on the wall of Huy Citadel in Belgium stating that: *The humorist P.G. Wodehouse was detained here from 3rd August 1940 to 8th September 1940.*

9. A Bit Of a Fixer

Nell was examining a newly arrived photo of Tom among the party of volunteers working on the dam. My, he looked well: lean and fit. He had been putting on weight before the war; he'd been so fond of the good life: restaurant meals and good wine. Now he looked more like the old Tommy, the young man she had married: slim and handsome. She looked at the photo through the magnifying glass, trying to make out his innermost thoughts. It was such a thrill to get a photo at last. Things *were* looking up.

In the accompanying letter, Tom mentioned that he had obtained permission to send Nell a parcel containing English books, courtesy of the Red Cross. He hoped that she would enjoy them. The one with the green cover would be particularly to her taste.

Christmas was coming – Christmas 1942 – and Nell had nothing to celebrate with. No money, no extra food, no presents for the girls. Nothing.

The parcel duly arrived and Nell opened it, the girls

chattering and buzzing around her excitedly. The arrival
of any kind of parcel was a very rare occurrence. There
they were, about thirty English books, mostly paperbacks
in a row, foreign-looking, exuding a pre-war life, a life of
plenty. They even smelled different. Nell's hand went to
the book with the green spine. She pulled it out . . . and
out fell a large bar of chocolate, a pack of twenty English
cigarettes and a packet of tea.

The girls gasped, and Nell burst into tears. What a
treasure! What joy!

'How did he manage it? Who did he have to bribe? Oh,
that Tom . . . he was always a bit of a fixer!' Nell smiled
through her tears.

Jeanne wore mostly hand-me-downs. By the time Marie's
clothes had been passed on to Irene and then on to Jeanne,
their as-new freshness was long gone. She longed for
something that had been bought especially for her, for her
alone. But she might as well have longed for the moon. She
always came last.

Nell had written to Tom, voicing her anxiety about the
coming winter and the need for a new coat for Jeanne who
was outgrowing everything fast. Tom-the-fixer wrote back
saying he had permission to send a Red Cross issue blanket,
and that it was to be made into a coat for Jeanne. When
the parcel arrived, Jeanne could scarcely contain herself,
hopping up and down with excitement.

'Open it, come on, quick, Mum, open it . . .'

There it was, mid-grey, in pure wool. 'Such quality! Real pre-war!'

Nell examined it. 'Yes . . . yes, that'll do nicely, and there's plenty of it too. Come on, there's no time like the present. We'll go down to the couturiere now.'

She put her hat and coat on, tucked the parcel under one arm, took hold of Jeanne's hand and they walked down to the dressmaker's at the end of the road.

They were let into the woman's front room that doubled as a workshop. It was an untidy jumble of patterns, bits of material, dressmaker's dummies, pattern books, a couple of sewing machines side-by-side on a long table, and more besides.

The couturiere spread the blanket out. 'Yes, that should make a nice coat for the little girl. Now, sit down here, dear.' She turned to Jeanne and cleared an armchair. 'Look in this pattern book, and tell me if you see the coat you want.'

Jeanne for once in her young life felt very grown-up and important. She knew exactly what she wanted. The well-off French girls at school, those whose Daddies weren't in prison camp and who could afford black market clothes, all had a coat with a hood and trousers to match. That's what she wanted. She very quickly found it in the book and pointed. 'That's the one!'

The couturiere looked at the drawing in the pattern-book and considered. 'Let me see, ye-es, ye-es . . . I think I've got enough for the coat *and* the hood. Now, what about the lining?'

A lining as well? My goodness, how exciting!

The woman showed Jeanne several samples of the shiny material, and they decided together on a tiny pink and mauve hound's tooth. This was very 'in' in the winter of 1942. Nell didn't mind paying the black market price for the lining material; they were getting a very cheap coat.

Jeanne was measured all over it seemed, then they were ready to leave.

'All right, dear,' the dressmaker said, waving goodbye from her door. 'Come back in three days, and we'll have a fitting.'

A FITTING! Jeanne was going to have a fitting, just like the beautiful ladies in the films. She hopped and skipped all the way home, bouncing on and off the pavement, singing,

'A fitting, a fitting,

That's what I'm havin'

A fitting, a fitting,

Isn't it excitin.'

The coat and hood when finished were everything she had hoped for. Jeanne felt so proud as she walked through the town on her way to school. She felt quite sure everyone was looking at her admiringly. She never did get the trousers though. There just wasn't enough material.

10. Radio Days

In the evenings, the girls would do their homework sitting at the large table under the only light, squabbling pettily in the claustrophobic confines of the only heated room. There was just the coal-burning, pot-bellied stove to huddle round. Coal wasn't always available and so when the coal ration didn't materialise, Nell bought bags of chopped wood and fed it into the stove at regular intervals throughout the evening.

'Your turn for an all-over wash tonight, Jeanne.' Nell had brought a bucket of cold water from the kitchen and placed it on the stoked-up stove. The water warmed while they were doing their homework.

It took hours to warm up. They never experienced the luxury of a proper hot wash, it would have taken forever to get really hot. No, an all-over wash at 8, rue de Monstrelet was not something to be enjoyed, but endured. The connecting doors into the bedroom were left ajar during this time, warming the room.

After simply ages, Nell felt the water. 'All right, Jeannot, it's warm enough now.'

Jeanne took the bucket of lukewarm water into the bedroom, closed the door and poured some of the water into the bowl on the washstand. She stripped to the waist, washed, dried and dressed that bit. Then she undressed from the waist down, washed, dried and dressed quickly. By now, the water was freezing cold.

When she had finished, she poured the dirty water into the slop-bucket, carried it through the sitting-room, making sure she didn't spill the water as she negotiated her way round the large table, went down the long hall, through to the yard and tipped the water down the lavatory.

Nell then cleared the table and brought the food down the bitterly cold hall from the kitchen. Mashed potatoes and boiled swedes again? War is a monotonous thing for civilians. After, they would stave off the hunger pangs with bread and jam, ration jam, that is. Nell swore it was turnip or swede jam, with a little fruit added to disguise the taste. Bread and jam without butter wasn't nice. The jam sank into the bread and it became a soggy mess.

It was at mealtimes that they played their favourite game.

'D'you remember, when we visited Uncle Tom in England,' Irene would start. 'Margaret his housekeeper cooked eggs and bacon for breakfast every morning. You could have two eggs if you wanted.'

Jeanne was incredulous. 'What, two eggs, each?' She just couldn't believe it.

'There were two sorts of cereal to choose from,' Irene went on. 'I remember, corn flakes and Rice Krispies –'

'Yes!' Marie interrupted. 'And there was a big jug full of milk on the table, *and* a bowl of sugar, and we laughed when the Rice Krispies crackled when we poured milk on them. Then we'd have hot buttered toast with a choice of real jam, with lumps of fruit in it, or marmalade.'

'What's marmalade?' Jeanne's memory didn't stretch that far back.

'It's a sort of orange jam the English have for breakfast. It's a bit bitter, not everyone likes it.' Jeanne could just about remember the taste of oranges.

Then the photo albums would come out of the sideboard, the precious photo albums Nell had sent for from Calais, together with Marie's bike. They drooled over the pre-war Christmas photos, with Tom grinning proudly while standing over a massive turkey with the carving knife and fork at the ready.

'My!' Nell reminisced, 'that was the biggest turkey you ever saw. It must have been at least fifteen pounds in weight!' Each time Nell mentioned that bird its weight had increased. That's what hunger does for you.

These games cheered them up. They reminded them of the other world, the world of plenty; that some day the war would be over and they would be able to eat proper food once more.

*

At nine o'clock every evening they heard the forbidden BBC news from London, given in French by the Free French. These broadcasts gave them the truth. They were an enormous morale booster.

Nell used to scream with rage at the radio if ever Lord Haw-Haw's sneering, mocking voice came on. He was William Joyce, the Irish traitor, broadcasting from Berlin, gloating over Allied defeats and German victories. It was all she could do not to take her shoe off and throw it at the radio.

'No, no . . . it's not like that! It's not like that at all, you liar!' she would yell, 'Our boys are going to win this war! See if they don't . . .'

Joyce was tried and hanged by the British at the end of the war.

Jeanne's place was by the radio. Being the smallest, she was squeezed between the table and the sideboard, and the all-important radio was by her on the sideboard. Sometimes, as the strokes of Big Ben reverberated down the street, they all shouted, 'Jeanne . . .!' and she hastily turned the volume down. There were heavy penalties for being caught listening to the BBC.

These broadcasts were their daily treat. They hung on to every word. First, there was a short burst of Handel's *Water Music*, then the V-sign was hammered out in Morse code: dot-dot-dot-dash, dot-dot-dot-dash. Then, *'This is London. The French speak to the French.'* It never failed to send a shiver down their spines each time.

Then came the news. Everyone in France was listening. This was the real news. They found out how the war was progressing in North Africa, or which German towns had been bombed during the night, and how many German or Allied planes had been shot down. There was absolute silence broken only by the occasional cheer. Jeanne wasn't allowed to speak until the news was over.

There would follow five or ten minutes of coded messages for the Resistance. These were entertaining and never failed to make them laugh. A solemn voice would say clearly, '*Mimi loves her little Choo choo. I repeat, Mimi loves her little Choo choo.*' Or, '*The nightingale flies backwards. I repeat, the nightingale flies backwards.*'

'What does it all mean?' Jeanne wanted to know.

'Well,' Marie explained, 'they're coded messages. "Mimi loves her little Choo choo" could mean "We're dropping ammunition at twelve o'clock midnight tomorrow at the pre-arranged spot in the Douai area. Be ready". And "The nightingale flies backwards" might mean "A plane will be picking up the four stranded Allied airmen from Soissons tomorrow at 2am. Be ready".'

'Oh, I see,' said Jeanne. 'They've already agreed what the messages mean.'

'Yes, that's right. But, you know, the Resistance are doing dangerous work. If they're caught, they'll be shot. They are very brave people.'

When the radio was switched off, Jeanne automatically turned the tuning knob. It was a reflex action, everyone did it. It wouldn't have done for a suspicious German patrol to find the dial tuned to London.

Listening to Radio Budapest or Bucharest in the evenings, Nell was very keen on a song that was played as the station signed off. She wrote to ask the name of the song and the answer came, *Lily Marlene*, sung in German by a singer called Lala Anderson. Soon, all the German soldiers were whistling it, and then the song was translated into French and played on the French radio. When the Allies turned up some time later, they sang it in English and claimed it as their song. Nell wondered how on earth the song could have changed sides!

Next door at number ten lived half a dozen German men. They were civilians, not fit enough to serve in the army and who had been sent over to France to work in factories. Nell never found out what they did exactly and didn't want to get involved anyway. The one called Frantz would sit at his bedroom window in the evening and sing and yodel, no doubt longing for his Tyrolean mountains. The good-looking one was Günther, all blond hair and blue eyes – a typical Arian. Hitler would have been proud of him!

Any summer evening a rabble of French kids would stand in the street and call out '*Brot, brot!*' begging for bread. Very occasionally a month-old army issue loaf would fly out of the window and bounce off the pavement right among them. Off they would run down the street fighting and arguing for possession. The next evening, a new ragged crowd turned up wanting '*brot*' and the whole pantomime started all over again.

One evening there was a real commotion outside number ten. A middle-aged Frenchman was shouting and arguing with Günther. He had to be restrained or he would have punched him. The man's daughter's name was mentioned and Nell put two and two together. Well, she thought, the young man might not be fit enough to fight on the Russian front, but at least there was nothing wrong with his male attributes!

11. Holiday Days

'I've got a surprise for you two.' Nell was leaning over the table as Irene and Jeanne worked at their homework.

'What sort of a surprise? Is it a good surprise or a bad surprise?' Jeanne wanted to know. She'd rather not have been told if it was a bad one.

Nell was bursting with pleasure. 'It's wonderful news. Madame Richemont down at the church says you two can go on holiday to a Protestant children's camp. And it won't cost a bean,' she added gleefully.

Jeanne was doubtful. 'Is it far?'

Nell looked at her eleven-year-old and sobered up. Of course, in the two years they had been in Cambrai they'd never left the town, not even for a day. No wonder Jeanne was feeling insecure. 'Oh no, it's not far at all. It's near Avesnes-sur-Helpe. It sounds wonderful. There's swimming in the river, and there'll be good food, and you'll make lots of new friends, and . . . and . . . you'll see, you'll love it!' she added lamely. 'Oh, I nearly forgot, Pere

Lacheret's running it. He'll be there the whole time.'

Jeanne's face lit up. 'Will he? Will he really? Oh well, that's all right then.' Pere Lacheret was her hero.

Irene said sensibly, 'But I thought we weren't allowed to leave the town? Do you have to ask the Germans permission before we go?'

'Oh, they won't miss you for two weeks,' Nell said airily. 'They're far too busy fighting their stupid war.'

So it was settled. Irene and Jeanne were to have a holiday, just as they used to before the war.

The Protestant children's camp turned out to be a beautiful old house on the edge of a forest. It had been a French king's hunting lodge and still bore traces of its former splendour. The large reception rooms with huge fireplaces and ornate ceilings were now crammed with long trestle tables and benches and used as dining-rooms for the children. Not an inch was wasted. Up the handsome sweep of the staircase, the once opulent bedrooms were stuffed with bunk beds, packing in as many small bodies as was possible.

The French windows gave out onto a magnificent stone balcony, which led down stone steps on either side into a once splendid garden – now neglected. Jeanne tried to imagine the elegant, posing, crinolined ladies sedately taking the air and awaiting the return of their men in the hunting party.

But now the garden was filled with excited children

playing games and shouting and yelling at each other, Jeanne shouting and yelling the loudest, her ringing voice heard above all the others. She was having a wonderful time. Here she had space to run, scream and be *almost* as naughty as she wished.

Recalling the holiday later, she remembered above all, the singing. Whatever they were doing, wherever they went, they sang. They were divided into groups, taking long rambles into the forest, singing. They learned to follow boar tracks and do bird watching. Deep in the forest, they even came upon charcoal-burners, who stopped their work to explain their ancient craft to the children. They also hunted other groups, using Red Indian tracking signs. They were taken to the river, singing, in a crocodile. The neglected pre-war inland beach, now deserted, still had a diving board and two dilapidated pedalos, badly in need of a coat of paint, moored by the water's edge. There was nobody there. The little resort was waiting patiently for better days.

Jeanne enjoyed swimming in the cool river, fighting against the flow of the strong current. Swallows skimmed the surface right in front of her. She even saw a kingfisher on the riverbank. He didn't move as she swam past him, but he had seen her, his eye following her progress up the river. Then, when her arms and legs were tired, she turned towards the beach and let the current take her, resting her tired limbs. This was so different, so peaceful, after the overcrowded, noisy swimming pool back in Cambrai.

They returned to the house in the evenings, ravenously hungry, and after the meal there was more singing. One of the leaders, Poulain (Foal), stood on the ornate carved mantelpiece and divided the children into groups where they sat and taught them canons and part-songs. They nearly sang the roof off! When they went up to bed, they copied out the words of the songs they had learned into notebooks, each one repeating and remembering the words, and then they fell asleep, exhausted.

One afternoon, when the weather was not good enough to go swimming, the girls were taken to the lawn at the front of the house where one of the leaders taught them some exercises, which they followed more or less enthusiastically. Suddenly the peace was disturbed by a commotion, someone came running up. 'It's Chevreuil (Deer), he's fallen out of the tree!'

Chevreuil was everyone's favourite. Charming, delightful, funny, he was very popular among the leaders as well as the campers. He had the habit in his free time of climbing up one of the trees with a book, and would settle himself there comfortably for a quiet read.

They all ran round to the back of the house. Chevreuil lay moaning quietly covered in nettle stings. The older girls cried, powerless to help their hero. A note was handed to Irene who was a trustee. She was told to run for the doctor as fast as possible.

When she arrived, out of breath, the Doctor's wife read

the note and gave a little smirk. 'All right, little one . . . Monsieur le Docteur will come as soon as he's free.' Funny woman, Irene thought as she ran back, wondering why she had smirked.

When she got back, Chevreuil's head had been bandaged in the approved criss-cross pattern. His left arm had been put in a sling, and they were now gently putting his right leg in a splint made of two lengths of wood and tied on with rags. The girls watched intently in silence as someone brought an old door from one of the outhouses. Chevreuil was lifted lovingly onto it and carried up the steps and they disappeared indoors. The girls hung around, not wanting to do anything except wait for news.

Suddenly, after twenty minutes, the French windows of the sitting room were flung open and Chevreuil stood tall, bandages falling off him. 'It's all right,' he said. 'I'm better.' It had all been a hoax – a lesson in first aid! Everyone laughed and peace and joy was restored.

On the last evening, they had a campfire. The children were again divided into groups, and each group entertained the others. Jeanne's group were 'blacked-up' as New Caledonian natives, sitting one behind the other to paddle a pretend canoe. They looked frighteningly fierce as they sung a native rowing song. Pere Lacheret was unrecognisable. He was bare to the waist, hair matted and his neck hung with beads. Most frighteningly fierce of all, he gnawed at a huge beef bone!

Irene's group danced a Spanish folk dance, wearing long

skirts borrowed from heaven-knows where, and playing castanets.

The next morning, everyone said a tearful goodbye, promising lifelong friendship and to write often, and Irene and Jeanne returned to their dull, claustrophobic life in Cambrai. Irene was asked to return to the camp as a helper – lucky thing. She had another fortnight there, looking after the younger children.

Jeanne and her best friend Nicole sat by the swimming pool back in Cambrai. It was early August.

Nicole said, 'It's the feast of the Virgin Mary soon, the fifteenth of August.'

Jeanne replied absently, 'Oh yes.' She was watching a girl being thrown into the pool by two boys; one was holding her by the feet, the other by the hands. The girl couldn't free herself, try as she might. But at the very last second she managed to grab hold of one of the boys' ankles, and he went in with her, splashing into the pool on top of her. Jeanne laughed. She looked forward to being old enough to play such games.

Nicole went on, 'And there'll be a procession in the streets, and we'll follow a statue of the Virgin Mary. And we'll all be wearing long blue dresses, and we'll have flowers in our hair.'

Jeanne heard her for the first time. 'What? You'll be in the street and you'll be wearing a long blue dress? Protestants don't do things like that, they say it's . . .' She searched for the right word. 'Idol . . . idolaters… or some word like that. Anyway,' she said dismissively, 'we don't believe in things like that.' She added ruefully, 'It's a shame though. I'd love to wear a long blue dress . . .'

'Why don't you come too?' Nicole goaded. 'Nobody would be any the wiser. They've got loads of dresses to spare, and they never count us –'

'Oh no, I couldn't possibly. I just couldn't . . .' Jeanne fell silent. What harm could there be? Just for once? She said quietly, 'Did you say you wear flowers in your hair?'

'Yes, and you carry a basket of flowers too. Come on, it'll be fun!'

It was the basket of flowers that did it – Jeanne could just see herself going through the streets of the town in a beautiful long dress and carrying a basket of flowers. 'Oh, all right then,' she said.

The morning of the 15th of August found her at a nearby convent. A nun looked her over. 'There's not much of you, is there? Try this one on, we'll see how it fits.'

The lovely pale-blue dress was made of shiny material. It slid onto Jeanne's small frame, landing just an inch above her horrid old shoes. The nun looked at her approvingly, combed her short, fair hair, placed a diadem of paper flowers on her head and handed her a basket of similar flowers.

'Yes, that'll do. Now off you go, dear, and join the others in the yard.' Luckily, Nicole was already there, waiting for her in an identical blue dress. There were about thirty girls, all similarly dressed, chattering and giggling. At the appointed time, they were guided out of the convent gates and joined, what seemed to Jeanne, hundreds of girls all in the same long blue shiny dresses, with diadems of paper flowers on their heads, and carrying baskets of flowers. They followed the statue of the Virgin Mary, carried through the streets on a plinth by six strong men, singing, '*Ave, Ave, Ave Maria, Ave, Ave, Ave Maria.*'

Jeanne felt wonderful in her long dress. This must be how the lovely ladies in the films feel all the time, she thought. No wonder the incredibly handsome men sing to them and take them in their arms and kiss them.

The procession came to a halt and someone blessed them. Jeanne didn't understand what was going on as it was in Latin. Fortunately, she had Nicole to guide her. Nicole whispered the responses to her and told her when to cross herself and when to genuflect. Jeanne did as she was told although she thought it was all quite unnecessary, a load of nonsense.

Suddenly, she froze. 'Nicole, there's Suzanne, my group leader from church. She mustn't see me . . . she just mustn't!'

As luck would have it, Jeanne was standing right beside a parked car. She quickly bobbed behind it and crouched down, holding her skirts up so as not to dirty them.

It was too late. The procession had broken up. Suzanne bore down on her, and the wrath of Calvinist Protestantism fell about Jeanne's shoulders. 'It's all right, if you want to join the Catholics, we can do without you. It's entirely up

to you . . . we only want good Protestants . . .' And on, and
on, and on she went . . .

How could Jeanne explain that all she had wanted to do,
for once in her life, was to wear a lovely blue dress that
went right down to the ground, and to carry a basket full of
paper flowers?

1. 1903 Wedding in Paris. Tom is cross-legged front right. Marguerite (his older sister) is behind him in a white dress. Bill and Jeanne (his parents) are back left.

2. Tom (standing) serving with the Royal Flying Corps in France in WWI.

3. Nell aged 20, a member of the 'Blackbirds' singing group in 1918.

All for now Darling
give a big hug & many
kisses to my dear Girls.
My kind regards to M.ʳˢ
outh & friends.

All my love &
kisses to you Nell.

Your loving husband

Tommy

Tom Sarginson
Prisonier civil anglais
Chambre 40
La Citadelle
Huy
Belgique

15?

Prisonier Civil Anglais
Chambre 10
La Citadelle
Huy
Belgique
6ᵗʰ August 1940

My Darling Nell &
my Dear Girls.

I don't know if you have
received any of my letters since
I left home, but this one is
about the sixth. I have had
no news from you, except by
Marthe Hut. at Lille & by
Lefeire with parcel.

Well we are been shifted
about; after Lille, we went to
Liège & you can see by the

---

still I'll tell you.
We have little to eat, but
are doing nothing, except
keeping our quarters & oursel-
clean, doing washing,
playing cards & reading.
We have the comardship
of others & that is much
better than at the first place
we went to.
As long you are OK with
the Girls that is the most
important, we can lump

Money I don't want.
We can not spend it &
ench currency has no value
in Belgium

---

address where we are now.
I can not tell you much.
We know nothing of the outside
world.
I hope it wont last too long
because it's far from being
amusing.
Anyhow we must put up with
it & hope for the best.
I hope you are all well
& still at home or if you
have had to go away, you
have done the best possible
arrangements.
I don't know what the
food situation is like for
you now, but you must
not send me a parcel

---

4. Tom's letter from Huy Citadelle, sent 6ᵗʰ Aug 1940, hoping for news of his family.

5. Circa 1941 Group photograph from internment camp. P.G. Wodehouse (hatted rear) is separated from the group. Tom is seated front right in his Polish cavalry officer's coat.

6. April 1941 The photograph that made Tom cry.

7. July 1942: Jeanne, aged 10.

8. August 1942: Marie, aged 16, on her beloved bike.

9. April 1944 Irene, aged 16

10. September 1944: Funeral following the massacre in Rieux-en-Cambresis

11. Tom Mahoney, Irish-American G.I. and comedian in 1944.

December 1945, a year since reunion. Marie was in the Wrens, Irene was a probationary nurse and Jeanne is at the front in her school uniform.

13. Jeanne (centre) visiting her wartime friend Claudette in Rieux-en-Cambresis, June 19

12. Friendship Days

Jeanne was sauntering along the pavement minding her own business, when a voice shouted at her from above. 'Hey, kid, get me some fags!'

A shower of coins fell at Jeanne's feet. She picked up the money and bought the cigarettes in the café nearby. She then went up the stairs at the side of the café and found herself in a beautiful room. There were things such as she had never seen: two deep red velvet sofas facing each other, a doll sitting on the end of one of them, her skirts spread out. Mirrors, pictures everywhere, it really was a most beautiful room. The woman was sitting in the window wearing a sort of Chinese-looking dressing gown and her hair was beautifully done just like the ladies in the films. And there was a wonderful smell in the room.

Jeanne gave the 'fags' to the woman, who gave her a 50 centime tip. As Jeanne turn to go, she spotted a large photo of a German officer on a side table with the dedication: *To my darling Mimi, love forever from your Fritz.* Jeanne froze, then turned around to give the woman a horrified look. She scampered down the stairs in a hurry with the woman's laughter following her all the way down the stairs.

A few days after the Liberation, Jeanne was shown a photo of a group of prostitutes, heads shaved and with large Swastikas painted on their foreheads. They were all posing and laughing, and it made a very strange, gruesome picture. It is said that they were very well treated by their German clients, showered with presents, and they missed them when they went.

Raymonde lived upstairs in the room at the back. She was a Frenchwoman, one of the First World War English army wives, and her husband was in the internment camp with Tom. She would come downstairs to Nell whenever she received a letter from George to have it translated. He wrote in English, but always finished with the same French sentence: *George-who-loves-you-for-ever-and-ever*, so George was not known as 'George' to the girls, but as 'George-who-loves-you-for-ever-and-ever'. Raymonde was the victim of many of their jokes. The girls spent hours talking about her. It gave them something to do.

'I saw Raymonde on her bike today,' Irene would say. 'She just looked like a witch on her broomstick.' There was some truth in that statement. Perched high on her black 'sit-up-and-beg' bike, her tight peroxide-blonde curls peeping out from beneath her pixie-hood, glasses on the end of her nose and a forbidding expression, they didn't feel like crossing her. She might have turned them into frogs or worse.

Marie would say spitefully, 'Have you seen her washing out on the line?'

Irene would throw up her hands in mock horror. 'Oh no, no! It wasn't, it wasn't . . . it couldn't be . . . Was it? *Bleu natier*?'

'Yes, it was. All of it, every bit, *bleu natier*!' And they all three fell about, helpless with laughter.

Someone, possibly one of her many admirers, had given Raymonde some parachute silk, which was difficult to get hold of and greatly valued. She had made nighties, underskirts, bloomers, blouses out of it, and dyed them all in a harsh turquoise blue, veering on green. This was the profound colour the French called *bleu natier*. Everything she possessed had gone through the dye-pot: sheets, frilly pillowcases. There was even a *bleu natier* silk rosette two feet across above her mantelpiece where the mirror should have been.

The girls relished it all. It gave them something to talk about.

Raymonde received visitors, mostly German civilians working in France and housed in requisitioned houses, all men together. They were too old or sick to be enlisted in the German army, but not too old or sick to come calling.

One of Raymonde's admirers was a small rotund man, with ginger hair spread thinly over a pink, balding head.

The girls called him Philibert, a silly name they felt suited him. He one day knocked at the front door and Nell, calling up the stairs, said, 'Raymonde, it's Monsieur Philibert to see you!' The girls, listening behind the door of the sitting-room, exploded with laughter. Nell returning, saw the state of her girls and said innocently, 'What have I done now?'

Marie, in a loud stage whisper said, 'That's not his name, Mum, that's what we call him. We don't even know his name.' And Nell joined in the laughter.

It was at this time that Nell's pony-skin coat disappeared from the hook in the hall. She was quite sure Monsieur Philibert had taken it. She was really upset, as it had been the only thing left to remind her of the opulent lifestyle back in Calais.

Another of Raymonde's admirers was a German soldier called Eugen. He was one of life's sweet souls, more inclined to poetry and music than to fighting a war. He became one of Raymonde's regulars. One day Raymonde, bringing down another of George-who-loves-you-for-ever-and-ever's letters for Nell to translate, also brought a beautifully illuminated poem written in old German script, surrounded by delicate pastel flowers and butterflies.

'Look what Eugen's done for me,' she said, proudly showing it to Nell and the girls. 'It's a poem by some chap called Goethe!'

One afternoon, Eugen brought a friend along. Nell was invited upstairs to Raymonde's room for a cup of coffee and introduced to Emil. After this, he started calling on Nell regularly. He was a big, gentle man, moon-faced, cleft-chinned, dark-haired. He was a firefighter in the German army but had owned a bookshop in a small town near Hamburg and longed to return home to his wife and his daughter Anna-Liese.

The girls would return home from school and find him and Nell sitting drinking coffee and brandy, two lonely people far away from home. Marie and Irene ignored him and would have nothing to do with him. He was the enemy, after all.

However, Jeanne was delighted to have a new playmate. They danced to the music on the radio, she with her feet on his big army boots, her nose level with his uniform belt, with the buckle bearing the motto, *Gott mit uns* (God with us). He laughed at the huge holes in Jeanne's socks. They spoke a pidgin mixture of French, German and English, Emil trying to remember what he had learned at school long ago.

He was a good man. He would turn up unannounced at dead of night with a sack of coal on his back, or a bag of potatoes. Heaven knows where he got them. Nell didn't ask questions, she was just grateful for whatever came her way. He also brought German army rye-bread, very foreign tasting, or butter – anything he could lay his hands on.

He became part of their lives, though Marie and Irene could not find it in their hearts to make him welcome. They felt betrayed, but there was no doubt that Nell looked younger, happier and less worn-down.

Many years later, when the grown-up Jeanne took elderly Nell on an outing from her old folk's home, they had lunch in Cavendishes in Cheltenham.

Nell reminisced about those long ago days, and Jeanne dared to ask a question she had had on the tip of her tongue for many years. She asked gently, 'Emil . . . he was just a good friend?'

Nell answered pensively, 'Oh, he was much, much more. Oh, I did miss him when he went.' That was all. Her Victorian reticence forbade her to say more. She sat, silent, then added after a while, 'You know, I saw him years later when Tom and I were on holiday in Nice. He was with a party of German tourists.'

Jeanne was doubtful. Emil had looked like so many other Germans. Maybe Nell would have wanted it to be him.

13. Visiting Days

Nell was reading a letter from Tom that had just arrived.

'My goodness!' she exclaimed. 'It looks as though the camp's on the move . . . they're being moved back to France.' She looked up. 'Wouldn't it be wonderful if Daddy was back in France? He seems so far away – all that way on the other side of Germany . . . He also says – and this is the really wonderful news – that wives may be allowed to visit.'

Jeanne stood up and shouted out excitedly, 'Me too . . . me too . . . can I go? Please Mum, can I go? I want to see Daddy.'

Nell sighed. 'Come on, Jeannot, be sensible . . . it'll be enough of a wonder if I'm allowed to go.' Trying to placate her, she added, 'I think it's very unlikely that it'll ever happen, anyway.'

In the winter of 1943, following many international negotiations, the internment camp was moved back to France lock, stock and barrel. According to the Geneva Convention, after a certain length of time civilian internees had to return to the country from which they were captured.

They travelled by train to the Vosges Mountains of eastern France, not far from the Swiss border, and a derelict French army barracks was opened up at Giromagny, a village near Belfort. As soon as they arrived, the internees had to clean out the barracks and make them fit to live in. It was freezing cold and their most urgent requirement was to keep warm. Anything, absolutely anything at all, that was not wanted was burned on the stoves in the middle of the huts – doors, chairs, wood lying around outside the huts.

So the men settled in and waited for spring.

The other most urgent job was to see to the camp's defunct electricity generator, and this is where Tom's skills were called upon. As he was an electrical engineer, he was made a 'trustee' and allowed, under armed guard, to go into the village to order his electrical equipment and all other requirements whenever he wanted. He was also put in charge of supervising volunteer electricians, and soon had the camp power running to his satisfaction.

Now that he was back on his own patch, speaking his own language, Tom-the-fixer became well known in the village. He even made friends with the local Resistance, some of whom were caught and shot during his stay there. Nell and the girls were mystified when they started receiving letters addressed to 'Mademoiselle Beatrice Marie', postmarked 'Giromagny'. These were letters from Tom, smuggled out of the camp and given to French friends to post for him. This was the first opportunity they had had to receive uncensored letters from him, and they could now learn how things really were in the camp, how he felt and his innermost thoughts. These letters were a joy to read. The censored letters had always been so guarded, full of veiled references and personal codes.

Yes, Nell thought, things are really going to be different now he's back in France.

The adjutant looked up irritably. 'Yes?' he said. A woman and child stood before him. Another annoying woman wanting something or other, no doubt. Didn't these people ever learn?

Nell swallowed hard. She knew it wasn't going to be easy but she wasn't going to be put off by officialdom. She wanted her travel pass and she was determined to get it, either today, or soon, but 'by jove', she was going to get it.

'Well, what do you want?' The adjutant said abruptly.

She explained. She required a travel pass to go and see her internee husband in eastern France.

The adjutant was exasperated: an English woman, asking for a favour from him? Really, what a nerve! 'Papers!' he snapped. When one couldn't think of anything to say, one asked for the person's papers. It was one of the first regulations in the 'How to be a petty official in an occupied country' rule book.

Nell handed him her British passport. He scrutinised it minutely, turning the pages slowly, looked up at her, then down at the photo, then back to her. Suddenly, something was wrong. He stiffened and took a deep breath.

He looked up at Nell, with her fresh English-rose complexion and button-nose.

'What's this? Lewis? Lewis? Levi? . . . Jew?'

'No.' said Nell wearily. 'Not Jew . . . *Welsh*. It's my maiden name, Lewis. It's a good old Welsh name.' She would have laughed if she hadn't been so scared. She didn't want to land up in one of those concentration camps she'd heard nasty rumours about.

He looked at the blonde, Aryan-looking child whose hand the woman was holding. He could think of nothing else to say. He sighed. 'Oh, very well then, I'll see if the Commandant will see you.'

The Commandant was pacing up and down anxiously, unaware of his luxurious surroundings. The news from home was bad, very bad. A telephone call that morning had informed him that Cologne, his home town, had been bombed – no, not bombed, plastered by the Allied bombers during the night. He was desperately worried, hoping his wife and children were safe. Was the war beginning to take a turn for the worse? His thoughts were black and troubled as he paced up and down, up and down.

Schmidt, his adjutant, showed in a woman and child.

'Yes . . .?' He looked up impatiently. 'Well, what is it, Schmidt?'

Schmidt hesitated. 'Excuse me, Commandant, Mrs Sarginson requests—'

'Mrs . . . Mrs?' He turned and faced Nell. 'How dare you?

How dare you!' He was about to explode. 'Your English planes bombed Cologne last night . . . My wife and family . . . How dare you request *anything*! Get out! Get out of my sight!'

Back outside, walking along the broad avenue, Nell tucked Jeanne's arm into hers. Oh well, never mind. We'll try another day,' she said matter-of-factly. Then she added, as she had done many times, 'At least we're not under the Japs, that's what I say!'

Nell was packing, getting ready for the hazardous journey. She knew it wasn't going to be easy but she could never have dreamed how difficult it turned out to be. She had persisted with her applications for a travel permit and, in the end, the Commandant had given in. He was probably glad to be rid of her.

It took Nell three days to travel to eastern France. This was in the months just prior to the D-day landings and the Allies were constantly bombing the railways, harassing the German troops and trying to hinder their movements at every turn. Every few miles the train stopped due to an air raid further up the line. The passengers were made to get off the train and wait in freezing-cold station waiting rooms.

Nell saw huge locomotives lying on their sides in fields on the edge of the tracks, like discarded toys, rails curled up heavenwards. They would pass non-existent railway stations, the name of the town scrawled in chalk on the side of a damaged wagon.

She slept in waiting rooms and saw Russian slave-labourers who were forced to work on the railway lines during the air raids and Indo-Chinese prisoners kicked awake by German guards. They were captives in someone else's war and far away from home. Nell smiled at them, and they smiled back, pleased to see a friendly face.

She finally arrived in Giromagny, a pretty village at the foot of the mountains. She checked into the hotel where she was expected. This was the hotel used by the visiting wives and she was able to learn the ropes from them. She found out that she would be allowed two visits, each two hours long, and that the guards weren't too obtrusive. What Nell needed most now was a long rest, a good meal, a hot bath, and she would be fit for anything.

She arrived at the prison camp gates the following morning with the other wives, full of trepidation. How would it be after three long years? Would Tom have changed much? Would he think she had changed?

Tom wrote the following to Gramp and Auntie Rikkie after Nell's visits:

I could hardly believe my eyes, she looked so well and perky! It is perfectly impossible to describe on paper our feelings and emotions after such a long separation, but it was good to be together again! We did not shed many tears of joy, we were so happy and it was grand to be cuddling again, oblivious of the censor and surrounding company of the visiting room – Nell is OK, twenty years younger! Yes really, of course she has lost all the superfluous flesh and dashes around like a two-year-old, alert, quick witted, just as loving and not a nervous wreck.

The women were shown into the visiting room. In one of his uncensored letters, Tom had told Nell to bring two large shopping bags. For the life of her, she couldn't think why.

The men were let into the room, and at last she saw Tom. He looks huge, she thought. He hasn't told me he's put on so much weight. Her first reaction was one of disappointment. He was wearing his large Polish cavalry officer's coat, veteran of two harsh German winters. He appeared to have a tiny head and the coat stuck out, forming a triangle, right down to the ground. When he hugged and kissed her, he was uncomfortable and lumpy all over. Nell was baffled, but she soon found out what he'd been up to.

After one of the guards had passed by and had his back to them, Tom whispered, 'Put your shopping bag between us on the ground . . . there . . . that's right.' Out of the depths of his huge coat came an assortment of tins, cigarettes, cocoa, jam, Spam, dried milk, dried eggs. It was the most amazing treasure trove. He was like a magician pulling rabbits out of a hat and Nell's eyes were popping out. She hadn't seen such luxuries in years.

Tom-the-fixer had been at work again. When he'd realised the likelihood of Nell's visit, he had bartered, borrowed, cadged, pawned, hocked, and generally made a nuisance of himself so that Nell would return to their girls fully laden.

During the visits, Sandy Youll, their neighbour from Calais, brought a tray of tea in, and Nell was delighted to have a chat with him.

As she left at the end of the first visit, swaying slightly from the weight of her two laden shopping bags, Tom whispered, 'Bring the bags tomorrow.' He hugged and kissed her goodbye, feeling more like the old Tom, not lumpy anymore!

When Nell returned to her hotel room, she packed the tins away in her cases. But now she had a dilemma. If there were going to be more tins tomorrow, how on earth was she going to get them home? They weighed a ton already. Then she smiled, thinking of her homecoming and the girls' astonishment when she showed them what she had brought back for them.

Just as Tom had predicted, the pantomime was repeated the next day. He entered the room, coat buttoned up to the neck and, once he sat down, tins appeared, just like so many conjuring tricks, and disappeared into Nell's bags. It was quite amazing. When they hugged and kissed for the last time and said goodbye, Nell thought she detected a twinkle in Tom's eye. There was something left unsaid, unresolved, and she left puzzled. What was he up to this time?

Tom was about to become a champion fixer!

The next morning at the hotel, a note was handed to Nell. It was from Tom.

It read: *Go up the road behind the church, keep going till you leave the village, go up the hill and wait by the sub-station at the top. Come alone.*

How mysterious, thought Nell. It just sounds like the script for a bad B movie.

She put her hat and coat on, picked up her handbag and walking past the church, followed the instructions. She left the village, went up the hill and there at the top stood Tom with a German guard, gun slung nonchalantly over his shoulder.

Tom unlocked the sub-station door and let Nell in. The German, smoking an English cigarette, stood guard outside while Tom and Nell, amidst the coils of wire and electrical paraphernalia, made love for the first time in three years.

The morning of Nell's departure, the hotel was buzzing. There was a rumour that one of the internees had somehow managed to leave the camp and had made love to his wife! As she said her goodbyes, Nell smiled sweetly. 'Oh, I wish it had been me!'

She left with two other women for the station. Their heavy suitcases were wheeled in a handcart by a porter. Nell realised she had a real problem: she could not lift the cases; they were far too heavy. The lad from the hotel had put them on the train for her, but how on earth was she going to cope when she had to change trains?

She found a simple solution to her dilemma. The first time this happened, she found a porter and offered him two English cigarettes as a tip. English cigarettes in occupied

France were more precious than gold, a half-forgotten luxury. The look of astonishment on the man's face was a picture. He touched his forelock and said in an awed whisper, 'Yes Madame, right away, Madame.' He picked the two suitcases up as though they were full of feathers and swung them onto the train, making sure that Nell followed him, and found her a comfortable seat. She had a good supply of English cigarettes and had no trouble in getting home despite the whole dangerous, miserable journey to be made in reverse. Stopping and starting, sleeping in freezing station waiting rooms, waiting for the railway lines to be cleared; when the taxi pulled up outside the house in Cambrai, she was exhausted, but she had to see the girls' reaction to the goodies she had brought home. 'Wait till you see what I've got to show you!'

'What? What?' They danced up and down, pleased to see their mother, and were bursting with curiosity. 'What is it, Mum? Let's see, let's see!' They crowded round Nell as she opened the first case. There were three simultaneous intakes of breath.

'Oh, my goodness . . . What are they . . .? Let's have a look . . .' They reverently picked up the tins one by one, reading the foreign-looking labels and exclaiming with excitement. There were things there they hadn't seen for years, and others they had never seen at all.

'But how did you get them? Where are they from?' They all spoke together, one question coming on top of another.

'It's your father. I've always told you he's a bit of a fixer.'

Nell then told them the whole story of her visits to the camp, how Tom had saved as much food as he could for them and of her difficulty in getting home. She told them about the porter and how she found that English cigarettes had made the best tips. She added, 'I think he thought I was a spy, or at least a Resistance worker carrying heavy transmitting equipment!' It amused them to think of their mother as a spy, or worse.

They went back to examining the tins, reading the labels out loud and translating for Jeanne.

'What's this?' Jeanne held up a large round tin. 'K.L.I.M.'

'Klim,' said Nell. 'It's American, dried milk.'

'Dried milk? Whatever next? I didn't know there was such a thing as dried milk. And this, what is it?' Jeanne held up a squarish, brown waxed box.

'Oh, that's dried egg.'

The girls examined the box in turn, turning it over and reading the cooking instructions on the side. 'Fancy! Dried egg! Who'd have ever thought it?'

Nell was well-off at last. She now had goods she could barter for whatever was most urgently needed, be it food or clothes.

Before stowing the cases under the bed, Nell poured the girls a cup of real English tea, with a little of Jeanne's milk ration added. Then she sat down, put her feet up, closed her eyes and took a long, slow drag from one of the cigarettes. She had earned a good rest.

Jeanne jumped around the room, sniffing the air. 'It

smells different, it smells . . . it smells . . .' She sought the right word. 'It smells English!' she said triumphantly.

Nell was to visit Tom again, in March, and this time she took Marie with her. The journey was just as bad as before, but didn't seem so, as she now had someone to share it with.

Marie, as usual, charmed everyone, everywhere she went. As well as her beauty, there was an openness, a frankness about her in those days that made everyone who came into contact with her warm to her. There was also her prodigious sense of humour. No matter how hard, how difficult the situation, she always managed to turn it into a joke.

When she arrived at the internment camp wearing a fashionable bright-red schoolgirl hat, she caused a sensation. Tom was bursting with pride as he showed off his lovely daughter to his fellow prisoners and all the men wanted to be introduced to her. His friends said she just looked like Princess Elizabeth.

Back in Cambrai, Nell had left Irene and Jeanne with Protestant friends from the church, the Pochet family.

Monsieur Pochet had an electrical goods shop down the high street. He and his wife were from Alsace-Lorraine, a part of France bordering on Germany. They and their five children, four boys and a girl, blond and blue-eyed, could have been mistaken for Germans, especially Madame, who wore her long, fair hair plaited and wound around her head like a German *hausfrau*. They bore a great hatred of the Germans, as Alsace-Lorraine has a long history of being overrun by Germany and then retaken by France, time and time again.

When Nell approached Monsieur and Madame requesting that they look after Irene and Jeanne during her absence, they didn't hesitate for a second. They argued that, since they already had five children to feed, two more would make little difference.

Irene and Jeanne paired off with the Pochet children closest to their own age: Irene with fifteen-year-old Jean and Jeanne with the younger ones, Yves, a little older, and Claude, a little younger than herself. They could well have come from the same family, their fair heads bending down over their homework around the big kitchen table.

Jeanne enjoyed her stay there. In the large, rambling flat above the shop, there was room to run or play hide-and-seek in the old cupboards and wardrobes and, what's more, she always had someone to play with. Irene was quite boring these days; her nose was always in a book. She didn't want to play any more and was becoming, as they say in France, *Une jeune fille serieuse*.

Jeanne always looked forward to mealtimes. Madame was an excellent cook and there was plenty of good food. Jeanne would have been quite happy if they had stayed at the Pochet's forever.

14. Bombing Days

Irene was down in the kitchen chatting to Nell who was preparing the tea. Marie was late coming home from college. Jeanne was sitting at the large table doing her homework.

Or rather, Jeanne was supposed to be doing her maths homework but it was all so boring. She had absolutely no wish to delve into the complexities of logarithms. She didn't understand them, and what's more, she didn't want to understand them.

She had written her name and the date, 27th April, 1944, at the top of the page and underlined them. She sat and stared at the blank sheet, then looked round the room for inspiration. If only, she thought, if only something big, something important would happen, so that she wouldn't have to do her maths homework. But it was no good wishing, she knew that she would hand in the blank page tomorrow, with just her name and the date at the top of the page, and it would be returned to her marked 0/10 as usual.

She started doodling on the page, signing her name and trying different ways of signing it. First JEANNE ELISABETH SARGINSON, which was her full name. But seeing it written out in full, she thought it looked like a bit of a mouthful, so she just signed JEANNE SARGINSON, which looked much better.

She warmed to her subject, creating extraordinary capital letters, first adding winding curlicues, then embellishing them with leaves and flowers and bunches of grapes . . . She sat back and admired her masterpiece. This was much more fun than boring old maths.

Then, she had a great idea. She turned her name round, spelling it backwards: ENNAEJ NOSNIGRAS. Well, she thought, that's interesting . . . that's really interesting. ENNAEJ NOSNIGRAS, the beautiful Lithuanian spy. Maybe she wouldn't be a film star after all, but a spy, dressed in a long figure-moulding crepe gown (not a dress, but a gown), in pale grey or pale blue with a matching head-hugging cap embroidered all over with seed pearls. She didn't know what seed pearls were but they sounded right. And she would carry a small pearl-handled revolver in a neat clutch bag, tucked under her arm –

Her reverie was interrupted by the sound of planes overhead. Jeanne looked up. Then she went to the front door and opened it. Yes, there they were, gleaming in the sun. 'Two . . . four . . . six . . .' Whenever people saw planes up in the sky, they counted them. Everyone did. 'Eight . . . ten . . . twelve . . .'

There was the most horrific ear-shattering sound, like a million planks of wood dropping from a great height. Terrified, Jeanne ran to the cellar door, yelling, 'Mum . . . Mum!' She never could turn the rusty old key, but this time fear gave her the strength to unlock the door. She fell down the cellars steps, sobbing, and shouting, 'Mum . . . Mum!' She had never been so frightened in her life. She curled up in the darkest, safest corner where the bombs wouldn't get her, praying out loud, over and over again.

Irene and Nell tumbled down the cellar steps close behind, and found Jeanne crouched down, sobbing hysterically in the coal hole.

Irene said drily, 'Shut up, Jeanne!' They huddled together in the dark, hoping they were safe; that the bombs would not reach this part of town.

After a while, Nell said, 'As soon as the first wave has gone over, we'll run up to the public shelter. We'll be safer there.'

Bombers came over in waves. The first wave of bombers dropped its load of bombs then turned towards home and there was a few minutes' gap before the second wave dropped its bombs. And that's when Nell and the two girls ran up the street to the top where the public shelter was housed in the local kindergarten.

Nell had grabbed hold of her handbag. It contained her papers. She thought that, should a bomb get her, her identity would be known to the people who dug her out. It seemed important to her.

At the kindergarten, they ran down one set of steps to the first cellar, then down another set of steps into the second cellar. They felt safe at last. A group of local people were already down there and a few heads looked up as they arrived and nodded in recognition. Two old women, all in black, hats on, sat to one side with their rosary beads in hand, muttering their Hail Marys.

Jeanne sat quietly, huddled up to Nell, with her thumb in mouth. Irene sat on the other side of Nell, bolt upright and staring into the middle distance. They could hear the muffled *crump-crump* of the bombs as they fell, and wondered just what part of town was being attacked. Old dust and cobwebs fell down on them from the vaulted ceiling.

A man rushed in. 'The college is burning!'

Jeanne howled, 'My sister . . . my sister! She's there! She's in the college!' She started crying and bawling out loud all over again. A few people muttered comforting words, but really they were far too busy with thoughts of their own safety to worry too much about her.

Nell's face was set and white; her lips tight and thin.

When the all-clear sounded they walked home in silence, Jeanne holding her Mummy's hand. Her tear-stained face was streaked with dust and filth.

They had no sooner arrived home than Marie turned up on her bike, eyes shining with excitement. 'My goodness, that was tremendous. You should have been there!'

'Marie!' they all shouted. 'Are you all right . . .? Isn't the college burning?'

'No, it's the railway station behind it.'

'Oh Marie!' Nell said, and sat down, her legs too weak to hold her.

'It was amazing,' Marie went on. 'When the sirens sounded, two of the boys grabbed hold of my hands and we ran across the yard to the shelter. There was shrapnel falling everywhere, all around us. Look, I've got a piece here!' She showed the others the jagged piece of metal in her hand.

'Oh Marie!' Nell said again. She was in shock.

That evening, after they had heard the bombing of Cambrai mentioned on the radio news from London, Nell said, 'Look, I've been thinking and I've made up my mind. It was enough of a shock with Marie and the college this afternoon. If the bombings have started here in northern France, it means things are hotting up. I think we'll be safer in the country. I'm going to see Pere Cadier in the morning see if he can find us a safe place. It could turn nasty.'

'But the Germans . . .?'

Nell went on, 'I think it's the beginning of the end for them, and what's more, I think they know it too. They'll soon be far too busy saving their own skins to worry about any silly rules and regulations.'

Pere Cadier was their new minister down at the Protestant church. He had appeared out of nowhere one fine day. At a meeting of the elders of the church, which Nell attended, he had told them that he was on the run from the Germans. His former ministry had been in the southeast of France where, sheltering and helping Resistance workers, he had come to the notice of the German authorities and had had to leave in a great hurry. He begged the members of the congregation for their help and support, to which they wholeheartedly agreed.

Nell went to see him the morning after the bombing. Was there on his books, she said, 'someone in the country who would be willing to offer shelter to a family?' He asked her to call again the next day.

That evening the whole population of the town, including Nell and the girls, strolled among the ruins of the station surveying the damage. They pointed out deep holes where familiar buildings had stood and bumped into acquaintances.

'Who'd have thought it? You'd think we'd had enough trouble here in the First World War ... What did they want to come and do that for? Do you think it was a trainload of ammunition they were after, or something?' The people of Cambrai conjectured and wondered, asking one question on top of another and getting no answers.

As Nell and the girls passed a huge German fire engine, they came upon Emil winding up a mess of fire hoses. He looked at them, and they looked at him, and not a flicker of recognition passed between them.

'Yes,' Pere Cadier said to Nell the next morning. There was an address in the country. He didn't know much about it, apart from that accommodation was being offered by some Protestant people and that it was six miles out in a large village called Rieux-en-Cambresis.

15. Rieux Days

As Nell packed a bag for each of them, her thoughts went back three-and-a-half years to the time when they had come from Marc-en-Bareuil. Was there no end to this madness? When and how was it all going to end? How she wished she was back in Calais, doing nothing more adventurous than spending the afternoon making jam with Clothilde and waiting for Tom's cheery, 'Hello Nell, I'm home!' The only thing she was sure of is that she had promised Tom that she would get herself and the girls out of this wretched mess in one piece, and that is why they were leaving Cambrai. Having got this far she didn't want them to perish in an air raid at the very last minute, just as the war was taking a turn for the better.

So now they were on their way again, not even knowing where they were going to sleep that night. What Nell didn't know was that the bombings were a 'softening' operation in preparation for the D-day landings, just six weeks away.

Her thoughts were interrupted by three men: neighbours

armed with large hammers. They had come, they said, to knock a hole in the cellar wall through to next door. If the bombings were to carry on, and people were trapped, they could crawl through the hole into next door's cellar.

Jeanne followed them down and watched as they knocked their hole – about two feet square – and then, crouching down, she could see holes in all the cellars going right down the street.

Nell called her up from above and sent her to the baker's to buy the biggest loaf in the shop. When she returned, the loaf was strapped to the luggage carrier of Marie's bike. Two more bags were criss-crossed on the handlebars. They each had their own bag to carry and Nell also had her handbag with her 'papers' in it.

They set off in the late afternoon. As they walked out of the town, Jeanne thought how lovely it was to be in the country. They felt like naughty children breaking the rules, leaving without permission.

At ten to seven precisely, at exactly the same time as two days before, the bombers were back directly overhead. Marie shouted, 'Quick, quick, in here!' and they dived into the nearest shelter. It was a First World War British army cemetery. They lay down and hid amongst the neat white tombstones – hundreds of them – in beautiful symmetrical rows.

As the planes made their bombing run just above their heads, two bombs collided, exploding in mid-air and sending shrapnel falling all around. Jeanne screamed. She was terrified. She lay sobbing, huddled against a gravestone, right up against it as close as possible. Irene shouted from the shelter of her own tombstone, 'Oh, shut up, Jeanne!'

They now knew what to expect. The first wave of bombers, having dropped their load, circled above the town. Then there was a lull of a few minutes, before the second wave grouped right above their heads and dropped their own bombs. They heard them whistling as they fell, right there just above them.

Jeanne was sobbing loudly. Irene shouted above the din, 'Oh, do tell her to shut up, Mum!'

Then, after a couple of hours, the all-clear sounded far away in Cambrai. The air raid was over.

They stood up, and as they dusted themselves down found they had not been alone in the cemetery. It had been full of people sheltering among the tombstones. They smiled at each other sheepishly, exchanged a few words, and went on their way.

Marie picked up her bike from the spot where she had thrown it in the ditch and they carried on towards Rieux.

They weren't the only ones on the road that evening. They encountered similar groups of people walking or cycling to friends and relatives, also seeking a safe place in the country.

A lorry laden with furniture sped past them and a voice called out, 'Marie! Marie!' It was her headmaster and his family. The college's proximity to the railway station had proved too much for them.

Nell and the girls were very tired by the time they turned off the main road and walked into the village looking for Rue de la Gare. Exhausted, they knocked on the door of number thirteen. A large woman in her mid-thirties opened the door and they explained who they were and how Pere Cadier had sent them.

She exclaimed, 'Pere Cadier must be losing his marbles! I was expecting a couple from Dunkirk!' Then, seeing their crestfallen faces, said, 'Oh well, you'd better come and see, but I warn you, it isn't much. Come on, follow me, it's next door.'

She led them to number fifteen and, opening the door, called, 'It's all right, Auntie, it's only me!' Unlocking the first door on the right, she said, 'This is it.'

Nell's heart sank. On the left of the room was a massive old-fashioned bed; in the middle, against the wall, a small cooking stove; and on the right, a washstand and bucket; in the window alcove was a table and four chairs. That was it. One room. One bed, for four of them. In comparison, the Cambrai 'flat' had been a palace.

Nell gulped, dismayed. She had no choice. 'All right. We'll take it,' she said.

Nell found that things were not as bad as they had at first seemed. She was used to making the best of a bad job and soon got into a routine.

She did not have the facilities to warm water up, but luckily the summer was coming, and they could wash in cold water. As in Cambrai they took it in turns to have an all-over wash once a week, the slop-bucket doubling as a chamber pot. Nell carried it through to the garden every morning, and tipped it at the base of the old plum tree just outside the back door. She swore the plums it gave that summer were the most delicious she had ever tasted! Otherwise, they were allowed to use the earth closet next door, but didn't like to intrude too much.

The old aunt lived in the back room of the ancient house. Her old frame was so wasted that she held a lamb bone under her right arm when she knitted, this acted as a prop for her knitting needle. Jeanne watched, fascinated, as the needles click-clicked, the lamb bone rising and falling in rhythm.

Rieux in 1944 was still an agricultural village, its main crops being wheat and sugar beet. Life had gone on unchanged for centuries. Nell would stand at the window and watch as two large, patient cream-coloured oxen lumbered up the hill every morning out towards the fields. They were yoked together, and lumbered down again in the evening, pulling a heavily laden flat cart. All of the farm horses had been requisitioned by the Germans.

'Oh look!' she would say, predating the Flowerpot Men by twenty years. 'There go Bill and Ben!'

Nell and the girls took to attending the tiny Protestant church just over the road from them. If the church in Cambrai had been small, this one was minute. It only held a congregation of fifteen or so.

Their ample landlady, Julienne, stood in the family pew next to her thin, puny husband, Jules, and their two small children. She gave praise to the Lord in a loud, strong voice that nearly raised the roof and drowned out everyone else's efforts.

Soon after their arrival in Rieux, Nell and the girls witnessed a procession coming through the village. A statue of the Virgin Mary, 'Our Lady of the Bombs', was being carried from village to village, resting in the village churches overnight. The villagers followed the procession to the next village, praying that they might be protected from the bombs.

The brightly-painted statue was carried on a plinth by six men and followed by the whole village, arms outstretched, barefoot, with their eyes raised heavenward in supplication, singing, '*Ave, Ave, Ave Maria. Ave, Ave, Ave Mari-ia*'. The Protestants decided that they should hedge their bets and join the procession, though they nudged and winked at each other.

Halfway to the next village, Jeanne, walking barefoot somewhere towards the back of the procession, noticed that something was wrong up in front. People were jumping in the air, stepping sideways and crying out. A non-believing joker had sprinkled tintacks on the road with a view to disrupting the procession. The faithful, still singing, were hopping about painfully, trying to avoid the offending nails. For a few minutes, chaos reigned but calm was eventually restored, and the procession went on its decorous way towards the next village.

Jeanne stood looking in the mirror, smiling to herself. Today was the tenth of May, her twelfth birthday. She was wearing a stripy, pale-blue dress, and liked what she saw. She felt on the edge of something . . . a beginning.

The girls soon made friends in the village. Irene had a friend from school living near the church, and Marie always had a string of two or three admirers in tow.

Jeanne was hardly ever home. Her particular best friend was Claudette. She was a weaver's daughter. This part of northern France was traditionally a weaving area. On rainy days Jeanne and Claudette danced among the now-silent looms, la-la-ing tunes, making up dances and pretending to be beautiful ballet dancers.

Otherwise they spent much of their time in the fields on the edge of the village. The villagers grew large mauve poppies as big as saucers, the seeds of which were crushed and made into oil. It was not as good as olive oil but it was oil nevertheless. Jeanne and Claudette helped themselves to the seeds rattling inside the dried heads. They tasted nutty and were delicious crushed between one's teeth. However, they caused Jeanne to be violently constipated and she had to stop eating them.

Josette was Claudette's cousin. When the very first new potatoes were picked, Josette's mother called Claudette and Jeanne over to the house. The three girls sat on the doorstep and dipped small, warm potatoes, still with their skins on, into a bowl of vinaigrette. They popped them in their mouths and the juice trickled down their chins. Delicious! Jeanne hadn't had French dressing for a very long time. What a treat it was!

In the early evenings she helped Claudette get rid of the *dorifores* (Colorado beetles) on her father's potato patch. They were pretty looking bugs, like ladybirds, but four times as large and with black and gold stripes. They climbed up the potato plants in the evening, ate the leaves, and the plants died. It was Jeanne and Claudette's job to pick the beetles climbing up the plants and put them into an old tin. When the tin was full, they took it to the path and either emptied it and stamped on them, or else set fire to the tin and watched as the beetles wriggled and writhed in the flames. As Jeanne looked up, she could see people all around, busy on their own potato patch, clearing it of pests. The French called the Germans *dorifores* because they helped themselves to French potatoes and took them back to Germany!

There were planes everywhere from one edge of the sky to another. The noise was such that Jeanne thought her head would burst. Where were they all coming from? Could there really be so many planes in the whole world?

The grown-ups were laughing and nudging each other. 'They've started daylight raids, they're not wary any more. They know very well they've as good as won the war!'

Jeanne thought the big planes, the flying fortresses, looked like whales and the fighters, hovering protectively around their sides, like small fishes, swimming about in the bright blue sea of the sky. The continuous thud-thud from the anti-aircraft guns sent puffs of smoke among the whales and fishes.

Then, there was a massive explosion right there above their heads. One of the whales had been hit and, in exploding, had hit the two whales on the other side. The air was full of smoke and falling debris clouding out the sun.

Now all the villagers were pointing and exclaiming. Out of the smoke and confusion two parachutes appeared. To everyone's horror, the first one didn't open and plummeted to earth. The people watching below gasped. '*Oh, le pauvre!*' Old women crossed themselves, praying for the poor unfortunate airman.

The other parachute opened and gaily, unhurriedly, swayed down, looking for all the world like the opalescent jelly-fishes on the beach back at Calais. It came down, gradually getting larger and larger, until it finally disappeared behind a clump of trees at the edge of the village.

When a German army lorry arrived ten minutes later to collect their prisoner, the airman and his parachute had gone. Mysteriously vanished, spirited away . . .

Three men had gone to work in the fields that morning and four returned to the village that evening.

Two days later, when they were walking through the

village, Marie and Jeanne were stopped by Monsieur Paul, the village policeman. He drew Marie to one side and held a hurried, whispered conversation with her.

'Go home, Jeannot,' Marie said. 'I'll be home later.' Jeanne skipped home, wondering what it was all about this time. The adult world never failed to mystify her. It was full of unspoken, secretive, unfathomable things.

Marie burst in late for tea in a state of high excitement. 'I've seen him! I've been talking to him!' It didn't take them long to work out that she was talking about the missing parachutist.

'He's at a farm near here,' she went on. 'A safe house. I'm not allowed to say where. He was so pleased to speak English. His name's Edward Torres, his family's from Mexico. He's petrified. You know Denain was bombed last night? Well, he was scared stiff. He had no idea what it was like to be bombed and he's been bombing people for two years. Isn't that a scream? I told him, "This is nothing, Denain's ten miles away. Wait till they bomb Cambrai again then you'll know about it!" But I don't think he believed me!'

Marie visited him every day while he was in the village. It was difficult to keep him in one place. In such a small community everyone right down to the smallest child knew exactly where he was, and he had to be moved every few days for safety's sake.

The Resistance were extremely well organised by 1944 and the villagers breathed a collective sign of relief when

Edward, accompanied by a Frenchman, left the village on an old bike dressed as a farm worker. At a pre-arranged meeting place they met a car with two other stranded Allied airmen in it. They would be driven to a place where, at dead of night, they would be picked up by a plane and taken to England, back to their airfields to resume their bombing duties.

The last they heard of Edward, he had deserted from the US air force. Had the bombings of Denain proved too much for him?

It was at about this time that Marie let it be known that she wished to be called by her English name: she wanted to be known as Betty. She felt it was more suited to the times they were living in. But Jeanne kept forgetting and calling her Marie. It was so difficult to remember to change someone's name after all these years!

Each time Jeanne offended, Marie/Betty got hold of one of her arms and twisted it behind her back. 'What's my name?' she asked menacingly.

'Ouch, ouch . . . You're hurting me! Leggo, leggo . . . Ouch, ouch!'

'What's my name?' Betty sadistically twisted Jeanne's arm a little higher, enjoying her power over her younger sister.

Jeanne was almost speechless and tears were beginning to spurt down her cheeks. 'Argh! B-B-Betty!'

'Right,' said Betty and let her go abruptly. 'Let that teach you a lesson, and don't forget! Next time, I'll really hurt you.'

Jeanne, nursing her wounded arm, retreated into a corner of the room, thinking, *Just you wait! One day I'll be as big as you, and then we'll see!*

On the evening of the fifth of June they listened as usual to the news from London but the coded messages went on and on – for twenty minutes or more. Nell's eyes sparkled. 'Something's up! We've never had so many messages. I'm telling you, something's up.'

That night, as they fell asleep in the large old country bed, they wondered just what was up, and where, and when?

'They've landed! They've landed!' Francois, the big farm lad from over the way, shouted excitedly through their open window. It was early on the morning of the sixth of June: D-Day.

They sprang out of bed, jumping up and down with joy and excitement. 'Where? Where?'

'I dunno yet, but they say Normandy, or maybe Brittany.'

'But that's just down the road! They'll be here in no time . . .'

They got dressed hastily and ran out into the road. It was already full of laughing, chattering people, reporting all sorts of rumours to each other and swearing they were true.

A single plane flew overhead, the RAF red, white and blue clearly visible on its wings. The girls waved and cheered at it. Surely they were going to be freed that day, or maybe tomorrow at the very latest.

When they tuned to Radio Londres that evening, they realised that it wasn't going to be that easy after all. The Allies had landed in Normandy but there was heavy fighting over a broad front, and it was going to be a hard fought battle. They now understood they weren't going to be freed that week, or even that month. They would have to sit it out and wait patiently.

Betty found a map of northern France and pinned it to the wall. She and Irene spent a whole day making and colouring little flags which they glued to pins: the Stars and Stripes, the Union Jack, the Tricolour, the Swastika. Every evening, as news of the Allied forces' progress was broadcast, they moved the little flags, sometimes imperceptibly, at other times a good half-inch or so, and eventually a dirty finger mark appeared in the area on the map around Cambrai as they measured and pointed in turn to see just how far away they were from the battle zone.

So started the long wait while the life of the village went on within the rhythm of the seasons as it had always done. Irene went potato picking, riding home on the long cart behind Bill and Ben the oxen, lolling among the heavy sacks with a group of laughing teenagers. Betty hung around with a gang of older teenagers, as she had done in Cambrai. Jeanne and Claudette gleaned. They picked up the stray ears of corn after the horse-drawn reaper had passed, more out of fun than necessity. Jeanne rode home, thrilled, on one of Yves Wallez's strong horses. Yves was sixteen, one of four sons who lived in the large house behind a high wall opposite the church. He had dark, curly hair and talked laughingly to Jeanne as though she were an adult.

Nell and the girls also played card and board games by the hour, just to pass the time. The table was placed by the open window, so they could wave and chat to acquaintances as they passed by. People stopped, leaning on their spades, or putting down their shopping bag for a minute or two. Everyone seemed to be killing time. There was much to talk about, notes to compare, rumours to argue over.

'How long do you think it'll be?'

'D'you think they'll want to free Paris first, before they come north?'

And there were tales of gun-toting, parachuting nuns, or a single US tank spotted down Avesnes way. It was difficult to know what to believe. The villagers referred to Nell, hoping she knew more than they did because she was English. But she only knew what she heard each evening, listening to the BBC just as they did.

So Nell and her girls played games, whiling the time away. Whist was their favourite; they became experts. Or they played *Nain Jaune* (Yellow Dwarf), a boardgame similar to Ludo. They used haricot beans as counters and, as the afternoon wore on, chewed them like sweets as they played, and at the end nobody knew who had won because the evidence had been eaten!

It was one such afternoon that Jeanne, looking up from her cards, said, 'Oh look, there's a German!'

Germans were a rarity in village areas, especially solitary Germans.

Nell stood up and put her hand at her throat. Her cards scattered on the floor. 'Oh my God, it's Emil!'

Emil walked slowly past the house, looking neither right nor left, and carried on up the hill as if he was on a Sunday afternoon stroll.

Nell waited a good half an hour. Then she put on her hat and coat, picked up her handbag, and followed him up the hill.

It was August. The Allies had reached the outskirts of Paris, and Emil had been ordered home. There, among the flat wheat fields of northern France, they said goodbye.

16. Joy and Sorrow Days

As August drew on, the noise of the fighting grew louder. They only had to open the windows to hear the distant boom-boom of the battling guns, slowly but surely getting nearer every day. Listening to Radio Londres was more important than ever now, though the flags pinned on their map showed them what they already knew.

In mid-August, there was an almighty battle to regain Paris. The Germans were not going to let go of the French capital, symbol of their success, that easily. The Parisian population joined the Free French forces under General Leclerc and Eisenhower's American troops, and fought street by street, building by building, until the Germans were ousted. It was a proud, emotional day when General de Gaulle, leader of the Free French, walked up the Champs Elysees and stood at the tomb of the unknown soldier, under the Arc de Triomphe in Paris.

Back in Rieux, Nell felt slightly disappointed. The flags on the map creeping ever nearer Cambrai were the Stars and Stripes, and not the Union Jack. She would have loved to have been freed by 'Our Boys'!

At the end of August, the sound of gunfire was really loud.

Day after day, bedraggled Germans passed through the village. The wounded and sick were carried on any kind of available vehicle, horse-drawn mostly. The rest were walking, dragging their feet, tired out and holding on to the tails of the horses. They were a sorry sight compared to the proud conquerors they had once been. The villagers kept out of sight as they passed by. There was no telling what a cornered, desperate man could do.

A lone German hid in a pigsty in the village. For him, the war was over. He had had enough. Sick to death of it all, frightened and shivering, he just wanted to go home. The farmer threw him some straw, a blanket, some food and left him there. 'It's the best place for a German pig,' he said.

One of the German soldiers walking through the village had left behind his spare pair of uniform trousers. He dropped them right there in the middle of the main square. No doubt, he couldn't be bothered to carry them all the way back to Munich, Frankfurt or wherever. Betty and her gang were sure the trousers were booby-trapped! If anyone went anywhere near them, the gang shouted, 'No, no, don't . . . they'll blow up in your face!'

Betty's boyfriend at the time was Jean Wallez, Yves' older brother. While all the others hid behind a wall, he walked up to the trousers and ever so gently tied the end of a piece of string to one of the trouser buttons. He walked back to join the others with a slow, measured step, holding the string in his hand. 'One . . . two . . . three!'

They all pulled together, and . . . nothing happened. They all collapsed on top of each other, laughing hysterically.

When they woke up on the morning of September 2nd Nell said, 'This is it . . . I can feel it . . . I know it is! Today's the day we're freed!'

Later that morning, standing outside the house, Jeanne saw a Citroën just like her Dad's pull up a little way down the road. Two men sprang out of it. They wore berets and scarves tied round their necks cowboy style, with the point at the front. They were the men of the local Resistance. With pistols, they gestured dramatically to the villagers to get back into their houses and then jumped on the running boards of the car and sped off with a screech of tyres.

'I wouldn't like to be there when they meet up with a fully-armed German patrol,' Francois said, laughing. They did look ridiculous, like bit players in a bad gangster film.

Then, a group of village lads called at the house, fresh-faced and smiling. They were going to meet the Americans, they said. Would Madame and the girls like to join them? It would be easier with them there to translate.

Irene had got up on the wrong side of the bed. She was in a foul mood, and she was quite adamant, she didn't want to go. 'I don't want to go,' she said, in a sulk.

Nell turned towards the boys. 'You carry on, we'll catch

up with you later. We'll be right behind you.' They went off, laughing and jostling as teenage boys do.

A quarter of an hour later, Nell and the girls set off with Irene dragging her feet. It was a misty morning. As they reached the top of the hill where the village ended and the fields started it was quite foggy. They couldn't see a thing. The boys were nowhere; they had vanished into the fog.

Irene was still reluctant to carry on and she hovered ten yards behind the others. Did she have a premonition or a sixth sense?

Finally, Betty said, 'Let's go back. We'll never find the boys in this, and anyway, old Misery-Guts here'll be happy.'

No sooner had they reached home and closed the front door than a German SS armoured car went past. The soldiers were armed to the teeth and ready to shoot at anything that moved. They were trapped, desperate and angry.

They disappeared up the hill and a little later there was a sound of gunfire.

Eventually, timidly, people reappeared in the road, wondering what had happened. Had the SS met up with an advance column of Americans and, if so, had there been a battle up there on the road to Carnieres?

A man stood at the top of the hill in the middle of the road, waving his arms frantically.

'My goodness, they're back!' Everyone ran back indoors and looked from behind the curtains.

A tank went by . . . and another... and another. There

was an unfamiliar star on their sides. They looked different. They were . . .

Betty and Irene yelled out in unison, 'Americans!'

The first tank had a name on its side: 'Betty'. They all ran out, yelling and cheering. Nell called out, 'Betty . . . Betty!'

And there they were, their liberators. The biggest, tiredest, blackest men you've ever seen – only they weren't black any more, they were grey: grey with fatigue, grey with dust from the country roads and with red-rimmed eyes. Everywhere, from one village to the next the same reception, the same ecstasy. Bottles and flowers were handed to them by the grateful villagers. The Americans looked exhausted and bewildered.

The people clambered up onto the tanks hugging the soldiers, kissing them. They had so looked forward to this moment, dreamed of it during sleepless nights: 'One day, one sweet day, we'll be freed from these damned Boche!' And that day, that moment, was here.

Bottles of wine were exchanged: those precious bottles kept all through the war years especially for this moment. A big grinning GI stood atop his turret and threw back flowers to the people below: a prima donna taking a bow! Jeanne caught one and put it in her pocket, to press later in her Bible. The church bells rang joyfully and the villagers danced, sang, hugged and kissed. 'Hurrah! Hurrah!'

After a while, someone approached Nell. 'Ask them . . . ask them, have they seen the boys?'

In a slow Alabama drawl, the tank commandant said

wearily that they'd seen several bodies on the side of the road, just outside the village, and that one might be a woman.

Nell's voice shook with emotion as she translated.

The jubilation stopped, switched off instantly. The mood changed in a moment.

'No . . . no it can't be the boys! There's a mistake. It's someone else . . . someone else's sons . . . Let it be someone else, oh God!'

The crowd went quiet, staring up at the commandant in disbelief as the bells rang on.

Nell asked more questions, wanting more details. Yes, there was no doubt, there on the side of the road, the bodies of thirteen young men. The lads of the village.

A woman screamed. A wild, animal scream.

All around her, Nell heard people wailing. No more joy would be had this day; this day they had so looked forward to.

'Oh no, no, it can't be . . . Who went up? How many? My sister… how am I going to tell her?' The villagers, with arms around one another, walked home crying. In such a close community, everyone was stricken. All had lost someone: a son, a nephew, a brother.

Nell was approached again.

'Ask if we can go up and get them,' the man said quietly.

Nell found herself on the tank, shouting down a field telephone to headquarters. 'The people want to know when they can go up there, and bring the bodies home?'

An irate American voice shouted back. 'I can't hear a Goddam thing! Tell them to stop those Goddam bells!'

A boy was sent running to the church, and at last the bells stopped pealing their joyful celebration.

Nell repeated her question and the answer came. It was not safe for anyone to go up yet. They would be told when they could go.

Yoked together in the early evening, Bill and Ben pulled the long cart slowly up the hill, another team followed behind, as they had done so many times before. They were led by a few sad men, their shoulders hunched, hanging on to the sides of the carts.

So the boys came home: two sets of brothers and cousins; one from the town sent to safety away from the bombs; Jean, Betty's nineteen-year-old boyfriend, who had been taken for a girl with his blond hair and glasses; his young brother, sixteen-year-old Yves with the laughing eyes who had given Jeanne a ride home on one of his father's horses. The youngest of them was fourteen years old. There were two fathers with them who had decided to join the boys at the last minute.

Bill and Ben, pulling the cart with their measured, unhurried tread, passed the house, and Jeanne saw lifeless feet swaying one way then the other with the rhythm of the cart.

When they had gone past, Nell said, 'Come on, I think it best we go indoors. We're strangers here, we don't belong. Let's leave these people to their grief.'

Betty was nowhere to be seen. She had known all the boys and the murders had hit her hard.

Nell came into the room and found her legs were shaking. What if Irene had not been in such a foul mood? What if they had carried on and found the boys? Would the soldiers have shot a woman and three young girls, or worse? Had Irene saved their lives? She reached for her handbag and felt around for her cigarettes with shaking hands.

Three days later, there was a communal outdoor funeral service in the main square outside the church, the ninety-two-year-old priest officiating. People came from far and wide and the square and the road around were packed. After the mass, there was a long procession to the cemetery.

It was at this time that two GIs turned up to collect their prisoner: the pigsty German. There he was, sitting in the back of the Jeep, helmet and bedraggled uniform still on, amidst the procession.

A woman, one of the bereaved mothers, became incensed at the sight of him. Another of her sons was dying of tuberculosis: his bed had been brought out of the house onto the pavement so that he might see the cortege go past.

The mother dashed up to the Jeep angry, furious and beside herself with grief. Before the GIs could restrain her, she took hold of one of their rifles and bashed it again and again on the German's helmet, shouting over and over at him, letting out all her frustration and bitterness. 'Take that . . . and that . . . You filthy swine! You German pig! and that . . . and that!' She bashed at his helmet again and again with the rifle. The man's head gradually sank into his shoulders; his neck had completely disappeared. He looked a pitiful sight. It would have been comical had it not been so tragic. The woman was pulled away and led indoors, sobbing and distraught, and the Jeep went on its way. The funeral procession reached the cemetery without further interruption and Jean and Yves were rested in the family vault, just a few yards from the graves of a New Zealand aircrew who had been shot down nearby.

17. Heady Days

About a fortnight later, Nell went into Cambrai. She wanted to find out whether it would be a good idea to return: if the college was re-opening and, most important of all, if there was any news of Tom waiting for her at the house. She hadn't heard from him since August 13th when he had been talking doubtfully about repatriation. Just a rumour, he had said. He was constantly in her thoughts. Was he still in France; back in Germany, in danger maybe? Or had he been repatriated to England? She hoped there would be news of him.

She also wanted to pick up a tin of cocoa from her diminishing store under the bed. She had promised it to the shoe mender back in Rieux. His seven-year-old daughter wasn't growing as fast as she should and Nell felt a good daily mugful of hot chocolate might help the little girl. Also, the shoe mender had offered a much needed pair of shoes for Jeanne in return.

She got a lift into Cambrai, taking Jeanne with her. They

found things unchanged at the house . . . but no news of Tom. After picking up the month's money from the Post Office, they walked up to the Grand Place, the main square.

These were heady days. Every day, a party day. Jeeps, lorries, Sherman mine-sweeping tanks with big chains used as flails attached to the front; all these and more were unceremoniously parked in the centre of the little town and were surrounded by GIs. They stopped overnight, sat in a circle and brewed coffee, for all the world as though on a camping trip in the hills rather than in a small, respectable town in northern France.

And always, buzzing around them like a swarm of flies, were hordes of local children clambering over the vehicles, begging for food, cigarettes, chewing gum – anything the soldiers could spare. If they were shooed away, another horde turned up immediately and the whole process started all over again.

Nell said to Jeanne, as they walked across the square arm in arm, 'You know, it's lovely seeing all these Americans, but do you realise we haven't seen one of Our Boys yet? Now *that* would be really nice.'

Suddenly, Jeanne felt Nell stiffen, and her arm was squeezed. She looked up. As if on cue, there were three of 'Our Boys' in RAF blue, smart as paint, marching across the square. She looked up at her mother. Nell was flushed and smiling. Oh, so proud! The miserable days of war were quickly rolling away and would soon be just a memory.

'Come on!' she said suddenly. 'Let's go and have coffee.'

They went into Le Cafe de la Place and sat down. There, at a table opposite, sat six or eight Tommies – British soldiers!

Nell, bright-eyed, whispered to Jeanne, 'Go over and ask them if they can spare some cigarettes.'

Jeanne crossed the cafe and tugged at the sleeve of the nearest soldier. She said in her best English, 'Ave you some cigarettes for my muzzer, she is Engleesh.'

One of the 'Boys' stood up and shouted across the cafe, 'You English?'

'Yes,' was the tearful reply.

'Where you from?'

'Brum.'

'Me too! Come and have a drink!'

Nell found herself sitting among 'Her Boys', speaking in her own language, not a foreigner any more. She was so happy, so emotional; her eyes were full of joyful tears. She told the soldiers her story and they listened intently, interrupting only when they wished to question her. At last, she said how anxious she was for Tom, not knowing where he was. She had no way of communicating with England yet. Civilian mail was not getting through.

The Brummie, whose name was Goodall, said, 'I'll tell you what, I'll get a message through for you. I'll write to my wife and she'll get in touch with your father and sister. They may have news of your husband. At least the forces' mail gets through.'

And that's exactly what happened. Good ol' Goodall,

as he came to be known, got in touch with his wife, who in turn got in touch with Nell's sister Rikkie and Gramp. Some time later he called on Nell with the wonderful news that Tom was safe and well in England.

Nell and the girls left Rieux. Back in Cambrai, the College Fenelon was reopening on the 1st of October. Irene and Jeanne weren't returning to the makeshift college but to the beautiful purpose-built college on the other side of the town, the original one that had been requisitioned by the Germans and used as a hospital throughout the war.

Irene and Jeanne were overawed when they returned to school on the first day of term, almost walking in on tiptoe and not sure whether they had the right to enter at all. But there stood the familiar figure of Mademoiselle Provino in the entrance hall, all in black as usual, straight-backed and beaming a genuinely happy smile to her returning pupils. She was back where she belonged and now had the space and appropriate premises from which to run a dignified 'gels" college for young ladies once more.

Jeanne, now in the first year of secondary school, was learning English. It was, at least, a subject she knew a little about.

Although Jeanne's English was poor, she knew enough to communicate with the soldiers. The Americans, tall, well dressed and friendly, had a seemingly endless supply of cigarettes and chewing gum. The English soldiers didn't give you gum, but they gave tea, chocolate, cigarettes and very occasionally, if they could spare them, powdered milk and eggs.

Most evenings, Jeanne was to be found hanging around the lorries, talking to the soldiers, American and English, in her funny, broken English. They were astonished to find this slight kid talking to them.

'Say, do you mean you've been here all the time? Gee, ain't that something.'

'I don't believe it, Sweetheart.'

'Your mother's English, Darling. How come she's here? Has she had a hard time?' Jeanne was hoisted aboard a great big British army lorry. A space was cleared for her to sit down among the smelly, untidy mess of war: shovels and picks, coils of rope, cable, wire, all neatly stowed away against the sides, and heavy-looking cardboard boxes, used as seats.

One of the soldiers solemnly brewed some tea in a billy can and handed Jeanne a steaming mug of thick, brown liquid.

Jeanne, aware that a lady is required to make polite conversation when invited out to tea, entertained the soldiers with lurid tales of life in Nazi occupied France. After a while, the soldiers went quiet, thoughtfully sipping their hot tea and gazing into the middle distance and thinking of the wife and kids safe back home in dear Old Blighty. They pondered on this little kid who, by a quirk of fate, had already experienced so much in her young life.

When the tea break was over, the soldiers had to drive on. Jeanne was gently lowered to the ground as they said goodbye. 'Here's some tea for your ma, Love. Maybe we'll see you on the way back, Sweetheart. Yes, look out for us!'

Jeanne skipped home, happily clutching a precious pack of army issue tea to her chest.

❧The casino in Cambrai had served exclusively as a club for the German soldiers during the occupation. Many well-known stars of stage and screen, French and German, had performed there. The French population had kept well away, apart from the prostitutes. Jazz and any form of swing music had been frowned upon by the German authorities. Viennese waltzes, accordion music and sentimental ballads had been the order of the day.

It was now the American soldiers' club, and the French girls they brought there heard jazzy big bands and saw GIs jitter-bugging for the first time. After the difficult years of occupation, these fun-loving young men with their different culture were as remote to the girls as men from another planet!

Betty did not return to the college. She was just eighteen and got a job as a hostess at the casino. Late every evening, Nell would put her hat and coat on, pick up her handbag, and cross the town to pick her up from the casino. Betty had decided that she was Marie again now. She thought it sounded more foreign and exotic to American and English ears! Two or three of the GIs, all madly in love with Marie, escorted them home. They stayed and drank coffee until the small hours, enjoying speaking in their own language and soaking up the family atmosphere. They would pass around photos of the folks back home and these were admired by Nell and the girls.

A month or so after the liberation, a victory parade was held in the streets of Cambrai. The whole population turned out in party mood, cheering themselves hoarse. Flags waved and bands played.

The British soldiers marched in well-drilled precision, putting Jeanne in mind of the box of toy soldiers she had left behind in Calais all that time ago. The Americans had their own individual way of marching, an easy-going stroll, quite unlike anything the French people had ever seen.

Loud cheers went up for the Free French soldiers. Exiled, they had returned and, together with the Allied forces, had helped to free their homeland. Many of the crowd wept with joy, there was so much emotion in those first few days of freedom. The loudest cheer of all went up for a small group of Resistance fighters in black trousers or skirts, white shirts with sleeves rolled up and black berets. The crowd went wild. How could they thank these brave people, many of whom had died in the attempt to free their country?

When the parade disbanded, the cafes filled rapidly, or people strolled around the square, examining yet again the army lorries and tanks parked there for the night. Nobody was ready to go home just yet. Tomorrow life could go back to normal, but for now the celebrations went on.

Marie had met Charlotte Pochet who invited them to come back home.

'Mum's cooking pancakes. She said to bring you all back.' Jeanne pricked up her ears. She loved going to Pochets, and she loved pancakes too. They accepted gladly.

Walking down towards the shop, Irene shouted out to a group of GIs. 'Got any gum, Chum?' She had been told by one of Marie's GI admirers that this was what English children shouted out at them.

A GI turned and said, in mock despair, 'Oh my Gaad, it's followed us!'

They walked through the shop and up to the flat. Yves and Claude were waiting for Jeanne and, as soon as they saw her, said, 'Come quick, it's brilliant! Come and have a look!'

They took her through to the sitting room. Here the older brothers, Roger and Jean, had rigged a mic. The children, giggling, took it in turns to sing into the mic, and could be heard in the kitchen. Jeanne really enjoyed herself and insisted on singing right through every song she ever knew.

Meanwhile, Nell and Madame Pochet were catching up on all the news. They hadn't seen each other for several months. Nell spoke of the liberation and the massacre at Rieux. Madame Pochet then told Nell that Roger, her eldest, had been picked up by the Germans towards the end of the occupation and, being taken by lorry for an unknown destination, had jumped off the back of the lorry and had run for his life. Try as they might, the guards could not catch him; he outran them all. How were they to know that Roger was middle distance school champion runner for northern France?

Suddenly, Madame Pochet turned to the older girls hovering in the background. 'I've an idea. Why don't you girls go out and get some soldiers? Fetch two or three, they might as well join us!'

Charlotte, Marie and Irene ran down the stairs into the street. Yves, Claude and Jeanne ran to the windows and hung out of them, egging the girls on by shouting instructions to them. 'Over there, look! There're three Americans, they'll do!'

They watched the girls run up to them and, with much laughing and giggling, took them by the hand and dragged them towards the shop saying, 'Come on, come on . . . we're having a party . . . don't say no . . . come on . . . this way . . .!' It took a little while for the soldiers to understand just what was going on, but eventually they good-humouredly allowed themselves to be led by the hand through the shop, up the stairs and into the large kitchen, where a woman was making pancakes, which were being eaten as fast as she could make them. Three younger children were running about excitedly. It was impossible to tell who was related to whom, they all looked the same, like peas in a pod. At the table sat an Englishwoman, drinking coffee and smoking.

The soldiers introduced themselves: a US army doctor and two orderlies. They sat down, accepted coffee and pancakes and chatted. Roger and Jean joined in too.

But the young people didn't want a lot of boring chat; they wanted a party. They took turns at the mic in the sitting room, singing all the hits of the day: *Lily Marlene* – in French of course – and *C'est la barque du reve* (when my dreamboat comes home), as well as *Music Maestro, please*. These were all English language songs that had inexplicably crossed over to occupied France and were claimed as French.

Then the younger children wanted to do party tricks. Jeanne remembered one she was particularly keen on. She and the boys locked themselves up in the bathroom, lit a candle and, holding the flame up under a saucer, blackened it with the flame. They then filled it and another saucer with water.

Jeanne went up to one of the soldiers, the one they called Poppy, a big friendly man, and said solemnly, 'I want to hypnotise you.' Sitting on chairs opposite each other, Jeanne gave him the blackened saucer and said, in a deep serious voice, 'Do as I do.' Dipping a finger first in the water, then making circles with her finger under the saucer and drawing patterns down her face, she chanted, 'I am hypnotising you, do as I do and you will sleep . . . sleep . . . .' Poppy's face was gradually getting streaked with black fingermarks. It was so funny, and Jeanne, trying not to giggle, heard the boys laughing behind her. Eventually Poppy was allowed to look in the mirror and see what all the laughter was about.

Then Irene told a story: the one about an old lady who has a crooked mouth and can't blow her candle out. Irene could usually spin it out for a quarter-of-an-hour or so, bringing in the husband, also with a crooked mouth going the other way, and the two sons, one blowing upwards and one blowing downwards. Eventually the neighbour is called in and puts the candle out with moistened fingers. But this time Irene had to tell the story in two languages and it went on forever!

When the party eventually broke up, everyone agreed they had had a wonderful time. The doctor promised Nell much-needed medical supplies, so difficult to get hold of in the early days of the liberation. She knew where they were wanted most.

Jeanne sat in Ralph Jones's jeep, parked in the Grand Place. She was chewing gum and was getting to be quite a chewing-gum expert. This one was a new flavour to her. Rather than sweet, it tasted of spice.

Ralph was a pleasant quiet American who bore a fleeting resemblance to Bing Crosby. He thought he *was* Bing Crosby and was always humming Bing's latest hits under his breath. He turned to Jeanne and said, 'Was there much barrel around here?'

'Much what?' Jeanne by now understood most English accents, but this one was different.

'Barrel . . . barrel . . . B-A-T-T-L-E . . . barrel.'

'Oh, battle! I see what you mean.'

Another lesson learned. She was catching on fast.

Ralph became a good friend of the family. He would visit whenever he had a few hours and leave them laden with gifts. Jeanne particularly liked the doughnuts he brought with a hole in the middle. They were quite delicious, and Ralph always brought a boxful. He also brought his best friend along, Tom Mahoney. Tom was a very tall, lanky Irish-American, a real joker. He had a beaky nose and a prominent Adam's apple. He looked for all the world like a friendly turkey. He was always full of fun and laughter.

The Americans based in Cambrai were giving a show for the schoolchildren of the town, and it was to be held in the Familia cinema, the large picture house down the main street that had been requisitioned during the occupation.

The children, walking in crocodiles, arrived from all corners of the town. They entered in hushed tones, marvelling at the sumptuous surroundings and the Art Deco statues around the walls of the foyer. Most were too young to remember when they had last been there. The pre-war days were so long ago.

Two GIs stood either side of the door into the auditorium and handed out an orange and a bag of sweets to each child as they went in. An orange, think of it! Jeanne sat down with her school friends in a comfortable, velvety seat, and ran her fingers along the surface of the shiny, bumpy fruit. She dug her thumbnail into the skin, and a smell reached up and tickled her nose. It was a long-ago smell of Christmas mornings and the joy and excitement of finding a stocking, full to bursting, hanging on the end of her bed.

There was a tremendous air of anticipation in the cinema. This was a real treat for the children: many had not seen shows in the last few years, and certainly not in such splendid surroundings. Jeanne was so excited she thought she would burst.

The curtains parted, and there on the stage, was the US Ninth Air Force Big Band playing so loudly Jeanne was nearly knocked off her seat. And such music! Music that had never been heard in Cambrai. The band first played a Glenn Miller hit *American Patrol*. The bandsmen, in Air Force uniform, had a stand in front of each of them, with 'Ninth Air Force' painted on it in silver against a pale-blue background. The bandleader stood facing them, back to the audience, beating in time to the music with his right hand. They presented a polished, well-rehearsed group.

At first the children in the audience sat open-mouthed. Spellbound, they had never seen anything like it. The glamour and glitz of Hollywood was here in their town. Not on some impersonal cinema screen, but right here where they could reach out and touch it. At the end of the first number the children clapped politely. Then the band struck up *In the Mood* and the audience, shyly at first, started clapping in time to the music, looking left and right to their friends, smiling, nodding, some even giggling. This was music they could relate to: a young, vibrant music, especially for them. At the end of the number, they erupted into cheers and whistles.

A sergeant stepped forward to the mic and sang, *'A-B-C-D-E-F-G-H . . . I've got a girl in Kalamazoo-zoo-zoo-zoo.'* Then came a new Bing Crosby song: *Swinging on a Star.* Jeanne just made out the words, something about a mule, and a pig, and a fish. She thought the songs were brilliant. She had to ask Ralph to teach her the words next time she saw him and then she could write them down in her notebook, the one she still had with all the holiday songs in it. And next . . . well, Jeanne couldn't believe her eyes. There was Tom Mahoney on the stage doing a mime routine of *The Lady Getting in the Bath.* He took off imaginary, delicate clothes and laid them gently on an imaginary chair, patting them down and carefully removing stockings one by one. He became annoyed when he snagged one of them on a nail. He felt the bath temperature with an elbow and scalded himself. Then he turned the imaginary cold water tap on, felt the water again until it was to his satisfaction and finally got in. Tall, gawky Tom, no one's idea of a genteel lady, brought the house down. There was a strong smell, a pungent, heady smell of orange peel and wet knickers in the auditorium.

Jeanne was beside herself. She stood up and shouted, 'I know him . . . he's my friend . . . he's my friend!' She first informed the children around her, her classmates. Then the rows around her, at the front, behind and upstairs in the balcony. Soon the whole cinema knew this, indeed, was Jeanne's friend.

Next came a couple of comedy numbers: men dressed as women, singing in falsetto voices and with well-padded bosoms to the fore. The audience loved them and laughed until they cried.

The concert ended with a couple of fast numbers. Two couples, with the girls in short skirts and bobby-sox, gave a jitterbug demonstration, the girls hurled through the air by their partners. The band finished with another Glenn Miller number: *String of Pearls*. Or rather, they should have finished, but the children wouldn't let them stop, shouting, 'En-core . . . En-core . . .!' The sergeant stepped to the mic once more and sang *Don't Fence Me In*, and then the concert was well and truly over. The show had been an unqualified success. The Ninth Air Force Big Band had never played to such an appreciative audience.

18. Paris Days

Nell held an important-looking letter in her hand and was quite agitated.

She said to the girls, 'Well, you might as well know. It looks as though we may be on our way to England soon. This . . .' She waved the letter, ' . . .is from the British Embassy in Paris, and they say if we make our way there, they'll repatriate us. We'll have to leave everything behind, of course.' She stopped, and then added dreamily, 'Wouldn't it just be wonderful if we could be home for Christmas!'

She went on, 'We can go as soon as we have our travel passes, we can be on our way then. We'll go to Paris by train–'

Jeanne looked up from her book, listening intently for the first time. 'To Paris? By train?' To someone who'd only gone as far as Avesnes-sur-Helpe in the last three years or so, going to Paris by train was the equivalent of a rocket trip to the moon.

Nell then said, a note of anxiety in her voice, 'And they say they'll fly us home to England from there.'

'What . . . fly? In a plane?' Jeanne couldn't take it in, it was all too much. Only rich people or troops flew, not ordinary people. And now, she, Jeanne Sarginson, was going to fly. In a plane!

'Yes, of course, stupid. We'll fly in a plane,' Irene said. 'How else do people fly? Really, you can be so dense at times!'

Nell had received a long letter from Tom at last, dated 13th November. It had been brought by hand from England by a Lieutenant Colonel in the French army who had posted it in Paris. In the letter, Tom described the horrendous journey the internees had undertaken.

The dreaded SS guards had moved into the camp soon after D-Day, replacing the guards the internees had grown to know so well over the years. Tom found that his trips to the village were curtailed. No more bribing the guard with English cigarettes while he visited his French friends.

The Swedish Red Cross had been negotiating for months with the German authorities for the repatriation of the old and sick, and ex-servicemen who had been interned for more than four years. Tom came in this latter category. When the Allied troops were only one hundred miles from Giromagny and approaching fast, the negotiations were at their most sensitive stage. The German authorities decided to move the whole camp back to Germany, the repatriates in one half of the train and the internees in the other.

On 2nd September, which had been Liberation day in Rieux, a train, fifteen coaches and seven wagons long, stood in Giromagny station. The men climbed aboard but did not leave for twenty-four hours, as there had been a collision further up the line. Luckily, the local Resistance had been informed that this was a repatriation or they would have made sure the train did not leave. Finally, to the cheers of the local crowd who had come to wave them goodbye, the train left.

The men, who had been locked up for so long, saw for the first time the devastation and havoc wreaked by the Allied bombers. When they reached Strasbourg the train, with one thousand men and guards on board, was stuck in the station during an air raid while the anti-aircraft guns blazed. The trapped men had their hearts in their mouths. They were relieved to hear the all-clear sound after two hours.

The train made its way through Germany and up to Bremen on the north coast. There, it was divided in two: half took the internees to a nearby camp; half, with 462 repatriates on board, was shunted into a siding and stayed there for two days and nights until negotiations were completed.

The train finally arrived at Sassnitz, a port further along the coast. There, three ferryboats were waiting. Tom was tenth on board. He was determined not to be left behind and had not really believed he was on his way to England until that moment. The crossing over to Sweden took four-and-a-half hours, during which time the men were given their first square meal in four years. They arrived in Trelleborg in southern Sweden, and what a welcome awaited them! Bands were playing and the Swedish Red Cross had turned out in full to receive them. Many were on stretchers and were taken directly onto a train made up of first-class carriages. The rest climbed aboard. They travelled through the night to the port of Gothenburg in western Sweden, people cheering and waving Union Jacks from windows and at railway crossings all the way, lights blazing everywhere, as there was no black-out in neutral Sweden. Count Bernadotte, head of the Swedish Red Cross, passed from carriage to carriage and shook hands with every one of the men.

At Gothenburg there were three liners to take the men to England. One was British, the *Arundel Castle*, and two Swedish: *Gripsholm* and *Drotningholm*. Tom was on board the latter, exhausted. The men hadn't lain down for a week and they all went straight to bed.

When Tom came to the next morning, he found he had slept in fresh-smelling, crisp white sheets. He washed and dressed, and wandered around the luxury liner in a daze. He looked into the promenade lounge with its comfortable basket chairs facing the sea, popped into the writing room with its polished wood writing desk and deep armchairs, wandered into the leather-upholstered bar, and finally found the dining room with tables laid for a meal on starched tablecloths. There were folded napkins, vases of fresh flowers and a handsome carved frieze above his head. And everywhere, charming, blonde, English-speaking stewardesses. The poor man must have thought he had died and gone to heaven!

The crossing took six days. A cheer went up from the ex-internees on the ships when the Fleet Air Arm arrived to escort them into British waters and the port of Liverpool. There a tumultuous welcome awaited them. Sirens blared and relatives and friends waved from the quayside.

In England, the repatriation ships were in the news. The Ministry of Health had broadcast a message on the radio to relatives and friends to write in giving a UK address for the men to go to. The men weren't allowed off the ships at once, first they were interviewed. Luckily, a postcard from Gramp and Rikkie was waiting for Tom and he was quickly released.

Some of the other men weren't so lucky. Petty criminals, who had been hiding in France at the outbreak of the war out of reach of British justice, were grilled by the CID and locked up again, this time in an English jail. Others, First World War deserters with two families – one in England and one in France, were marched off under armed escort.

Gramp and Rikkie welcomed Tom home with open arms. Bewildered and dazed, Tom rested at Gramps's for a fortnight. He had half hoped Nell and the girls would be waiting to welcome him when he arrived, but it wasn't to be.

He still had no news and didn't know what had happened to them. Every day, he sent two postcards; one to Rieux and one to Cambrai. He didn't hear from them until September 29th, through a Gunner named Woodward. Then, almost immediately after that, news came via Good Ol' Goodall's wife.

Meanwhile, he and Rikkie had begun badgering the Foreign Office in London, writing to them most days to request Nell and the girls' repatriation.

Tom then approached Courtaulds, his old firm, asking whether he could return to work. He was interviewed three times to assess his state of mind. In December 1944, at the age of forty-seven, Tom was being retrained at the Courtaulds Preston factory.

Jeanne stood in the corridor, looking out of the train window and watching fields, rivers and villages speeding past, sometimes obliterated by the smoke pouring out of the train engine's funnel. Nell shouted from the inner carriage's open door. 'Shut the window quick, Jeannot! There's a draught! I'm getting covered with smuts from the smoke!' Jeanne did as she was told, though she couldn't see so clearly now, as the train windows were all steamed up and dirty. They were on the outskirts of Peronne, going over a river. The rain slowed down to a snail's pace.

A man sitting opposite Nell in the carriage, said, 'They're having to go slowly here. The bridge was blown up by the Resistance just before the liberation and this bridge is only temporary.' Jeanne was impressed. She looked down from the window expecting to be plunged any moment into the foaming river below and swept away in the raging torrent, but not before she had rescued her mother, her two sisters and their luggage.

They were on their way again, gathering speed. Jeanne went back to her musing at her place by the window. That woman, hanging out her washing in her back garden just by the railway line: had she ever been to Paris by train, as Jeanne was doing now? Or did she just plan her life's routine to the railway timetable? Did the 07.30 coming up from Paris, for example, mean it was time to wake her children up for school? And when the 11.30 from Lille sped through on its way down, was it time to put the lunchtime soup on the stove? Why, thought Jeanne, if you lived by a railway line, you didn't even need to own a clock.

When they went through Creil, an important railway junction just north of Paris, there was evidence of heavy bombing, such as Nell and Marie had encountered on their visits to Tom. Nell had described it, but it was the first time that Jeanne and Irene had actually seen it. Marie and Irene joined Jeanne at the window and looked out in disbelief. Mile upon mile of railway tracks, and buildings surrounding the tracks, were devastated. They simply did not exist any more. It was as though a giant had pounded the area with a huge fist over and over again. Many of the railway lines were out of action and it seemed as though theirs was the only serviceable one.

After Creil, they made their way slowly, oh, ever so slowly, into the capital. And then, just when Jeanne thought she would die of boredom, they were there. The girls picked up their bags, Nell her case and her handbag with her papers, and found their way out of the Gare du Nord. The people . . . the tall buildings . . . the noise . . . Jeanne stood transfixed. It was all so much bigger, brighter, and louder than she had expected. She stood open-mouthed. Irene shouted, 'Come on, Jeanne, you'll lose us!' She ran to catch them up. Nell and Marie were planning their next move. As usual, Nell had very little money.

Marie said, 'I saw a woman with a Red Cross armband in the station. Maybe she can give us the address of a cheap hotel?' They went back into the main hall, a turmoil of post-liberation chaos. People were returning home from far away, their only belongings in cardboard-boxes tied up with string. There were soldiers and airmen: British, French, American; British Redcaps (military police), US military police also — nicknamed 'Snowdrops' because they wore white helmets — French civilian police, smartly dressed commuters; all getting in each other's way, pushing, shoving, jostling.

Marie suggested, 'Look, we'll never find her in this crowd. Mum, you stay here with Irene and Jeannot, and I'll go and find her.' Marie disappeared and returned twenty minutes later. Nell and the others were waiting where she had left them, sitting on their bags.

'It's almost impossible,' she said. 'There's hardly anything available at all. She's given me an address, it's down by the Seine. Come on, I've found the Metro entrance.' They followed her, Jeanne trudging behind making sure she didn't lose sight of them. She could get lost in this crowd for a week, she thought, and not be found.

They came out of the Metro in a seedy area alongside the River Seine. They ate in a cheap cafe and, armed with directions, found the house the Red Cross worker had recommended.

Nell's heart, not for the first time in all their adventures, sank. 'Why,' she said, 'it's a dosshouse! It's where the tramps come for a sleep and a warm up.' She turned and faced her daughters. 'Look, we've got no choice. It's getting late and we're tired out. We'll stay here just for tonight. I promise you, just for one night. Tomorrow, we'll think of something else. I'm sure we can think of something better than this.' And that's what they did. Nell, seeing the condition of the old mattresses on the iron bedsteads, made the girls roll themselves up in their coats, so they wouldn't catch anything. Then she propped herself up against the wall. Half sitting and rolled up in her own coat she stood guard over her daughters all night. Jeanne fell exhaustedly asleep to a symphony of coughing, snoring and farting.

The next morning found them back in the cafe, dirty, dishevelled, and dusty. They dipped hunks of jammy baguette in their bowls of coffee. Nell, Marie and Irene were arguing, trying to decide what they should do next.

Irene said emphatically, 'Well, we're not going back there tonight. Phew . . . don't those men whiff! I thought I'd be sick!'

Marie chipped in, 'Why don't we go and see if Gaston and Jeanne are still there?'

'Oh no, we couldn't possibly,' Nell remonstrated. 'There's four of us, it'd be too much of an imposition.'

Bill Sarginson's best friend throughout the Naughty Nineties and into the new century had been Gaston Baurain. Gaston was now an old man, living with his wife in retirement in Paris.

Marie went on, 'Oh, come on, they can only say no. Or they might at least know someone who could put us up.'

Nell sighed. 'Oh, all right then.' There was no arguing with Marie. Once she had a bee in her bonnet about something she was unstoppable. Nell fished in the depths of her handbag and found a battered old address book. 'There you are.' She had found the right page. 'Rue Cernuschi.'

Marie and Irene got up from the table and looked at the map of Paris pinned on the wall with rusty drawing pins, among adverts for Pernod and football fixture notices.

'Here we are!' Irene found it. 'Paris XVII, by Avenue Wagram.'

The cafe owner, busy polishing glasses with a dirty cloth, was impressed. 'Avenue Wagram? My goodness, you're going to a posh area and no mistake!'

'Come on then, let's go!' Marie, now she had the idea in mind, wanted it carried out instantly.

They came out of the Metro in an exclusive part of Paris, not far from the Arc de Triomphe. They were in an avenue typical of central Paris, lined with elegant old apartment buildings stretching skywards.

Nell felt unkempt and wondered how their old friends would receive them. It wouldn't have been so bad if they could have telephoned first, but all the telephones were still out of action since the liberation.

She need not have worried.

They entered through the large front door of number seventeen and, on the first floor, rang the bell. An elderly maid answered the door, and there, behind her, was an old couple.

'Nellie! Nellie, my dear . . . and your lovely girls! What a wonderful surprise! Come in, come in! Why, you poor things, you do look as though you've had a rough journey. And Tommy, have you heard from him?' Gaston and his wife Jeanne both spoke at the same time. Turning to the maid hovering in the doorway, Gaston called, 'Hortense, coffee please for the ladies,' then to Nell, 'Now, Nellie, come and sit down, we want to hear all your news...' Seeing Jeanne by the door, he said, 'Yes, go on in! Now, which one are you? Yes, Jeanne, that's right, I remember. Go on, Dear, you may explore the flat.'

Jeanne wandered down the hall of the large flat, attracted by the tantalising cooking smells. She found the kitchen, pristine-clean, with rows of graduated shiny pans hanging on the wall. Hortense was sitting with a coffee mill on her lap, grinding the coffee grains. She looked up and smiled and Jeanne watched her. Hortense, satisfied she had enough, pulled out the full drawer beneath the grinder, measured the scented coffee into the coffee pot and poured boiling water over it. The combined aroma of freshly ground coffee and Boeuf Bourguignon was almost unbearable. It smelled so good!

Jeanne carried on with her tour of inspection, looking around bedroom doors into rooms full of old-fashioned, highly polished furniture. There were carved wardrobes with matching dressing tables, and high beds you had to climb into.

At the end of the hall, she found what she was looking for – *the bathroom*. This was a real, genuine bathroom: deep pink, the sort dreams are made of – straight out of a film! There was a deep bath, she would lose her footing if she should overfill it, and a matching washbasin. She ran her fingers along the bath almost afraid to touch, then gingerly turned on the hot tap, trying not to make a noise. A stream of hot water gushed out. When had she last had a bath, a proper bath? She couldn't remember. It was so long ago. She dimly recalled playing for hours with the suds. She used to form a triangle, with thumbs and forefingers joined, trying to blow the biggest bubble in the world.

Beyond the bath was a pink WC, with a chain hanging from the high cistern. Not a smelly, squatting Turkish lavatory, the sort that soaked her feet if she didn't jump out of the way quickly when she pushed the flushing handle on the wall, nor an earth closet with the wind swirling round from underneath, chilling her nether-regions, nor the lever-type stinking lavatory in the back yard in Cambrai. No, this was a proper WC, with a warm, wooden seat and a proper roll of toilet paper close at hand; the sort she would like to sit on comfortably and have a quiet read for twenty minutes or so.

Irene caught up with her, brimming with excitement. 'Looks as though we're staying here!'

Jeanne said, quick as a flash, 'Me first with the bathroom!'

The British Embassy in the Avenue Friedland was besieged with crowds of people laying claim to British citizenship and clamouring to be given priority for repatriation to Britain. It was total confusion and mayhem.

Nell, after a wait of several hours, finally took her turn at the desk in front of the harassed official, clutching her all-important dark blue British passport and the letter she had received from the Embassy.

'Ah yes.' The official looked up from a mound of papers after spending several minutes selecting the appropriate ones. 'Mrs Sarginson, you and your children have top priority. You will be on the first repatriation plane, as soon as it can be organised.' He added with a sigh, 'Your husband and a Miss Lewis have been in touch with the Foreign Office in London several times on your behalf.'

Nell smiled. Good old Tom and Rikkie, they had been busy!

The tired official went on, 'Please present yourselves here each morning, and we'll do our utmost.'

Nell asked anxiously, 'Do you think we'll be home for Christmas?'

The official smiled wanly. 'We're doing our utmost . . .' He called out, 'Next please!'

And so a routine was established. Nell and the girls would leave the comfort of Gaston and Jeanne's flat each morning to join the daily chaos at the British Embassy. They sat all day long, the girls bored stiff, in a long corridor full of anxious people, and at the end of the day were sent away and told to return the following morning. This routine went on for several days.

On the Sunday, they visited Suzanne.

Bill Sarginson's wife Jeanne had a sister, Marie, who was married to an artist, Henri d'Estienne, and Suzanne was their only daughter. In 1944, Suzanne was in her mid-forties, a strikingly handsome Spanish-looking woman. She had wanted to become an artist, but had been married off to a count by her father, who feared a rival. The marriage was an unhappy one, and Suzanne and her husband were barely civil to one another.

She lived in an apartment overlooking the little square at St. Germain-des-Pres, the centre of left-bank intellectualism. She was an avid theatre and concert goer and her nearest neighbour was Jean-Paul Sartre, the left-wing writer. She opposed his philosophies and it was all she could do to exchange greetings when she met him on the stairs with his long-time mistress, the feminist writer Simone de Beauvoir.

In her sitting room overlooking the square, that Sunday afternoon in December 1944, the walls covered with her father's exquisite paintings and pastels, Suzanne entertained Nell and the girls by playing Bach on the piano. Marie was in her element, chatting to Suzanne about various composers, following the music and turning the pages for her, but Irene and Jeanne were bored to tears and starving hungry.

In the late afternoon, still without food, Suzanne suggested they should go to a soiree friends of hers were holding that evening. They went by taxi, an unheard-of luxury to the girls, and stopped outside a *porte-cochere*, one of those wide, anonymous doorways that are prevalent in French towns. The door opened, and on the doorstep was the most extraordinary sight they had ever encountered.

Smiling benignly, an old man welcomed them in. He was dressed in a white, flowing Roman toga, leather sandals on his bare feet, and his long grey hair hung down in two thin plaits, resting on his shoulders.

Suzanne kissed him warmly and introduced him as Raymond Duncan, an American. Nell knew at once this was *the* Raymond Duncan, brother of the famed dancer, Isadora.

Isadora Duncan was known as 'the Mother of Modern Dance'. At the turn of the century, she evolved a free style, taking dance back to its beginnings. In 1903, she travelled to Greece in her search for a perfect dance form. She believed she would find her answer within the ruins of Ancient Greece. Her family followed her and, deciding to build an Art Commune, they bought a hill site at Kopanos. Raymond drew up plans to include a house, a small temple, a Greek theatre and a library. But the project ran out of money and was abandoned. It was clear that Isadora was not made for the simple life. She left Kopanos and went to find fame and fortune throughout the theatres and concert halls of Europe. She died when the long scarf she was wearing became entangled in the wheel of the car driven by her latest lover. She had been enormously influential, forcing dancers to re-appraise the techniques of the time.

Raymond was the only Duncan to remain true to the family's ideal of an aesthetic life.

Next to Raymond were two uniformed GIs, one of whom he introduced as his nephew. Nell wondered whether this could be Isadora's son, or maybe Isadora's sister Laura's.

A tall man in a long black tailed coat and shirt with starched wing collar, gushed forward. '*Cherie Anglaise!*' He took hold of Nell's hand and kissed it.

Nell blushed delightedly. She felt the years of hardship rolling away. This was more like it, she thought.

They were led through into a small concert hall within the house. A grand piano stood on the stage and facing it were twenty-five to thirty chairs arranged in a semi-circle.

The gusher in the tailed coat stepped onto the stage

and, bowing and acknowledging the applause of the small, select audience, took his shoes off. Suzanne whispered to Nell that he was a pupil of the great Alfred Cortot and he always played in his stocking feet!

He started to play a Chopin etude. Marie sat, bending forward, enraptured. Waves of boredom and hunger swept over Jeanne once more, and she slumped into her chair.

Much later in the 1960s, the O.A.S group that opposed Algerian independence from France, placed a plastic bomb in the stairwell of the block of flats where Jean-Paul Sartre lived. He was away, but Suzanne's apartment on the floor below received the full force of the explosion. Luckily she was in the kitchen at the back of the building, or she would have been killed. In a frantic letter to Cousin Tom telling him about the incident, she told how she had to use the service stairs for months, during the repairs to the building.

The next day, they visited Suzanne's parents: their Great Aunt Marie and her artist husband, Henri d'Estienne, who had gained some success in his youth. At the turn of the century, he had won the Prix de Rome and had had a triptych, *Noces Bretonne*, (Breton Wedding) hung over the staircase of the Louvre. With his prize money he had travelled to Algeria and had painted exquisite portraits of Algerian women in all their finery. He had said laughing, that their husbands would sit in the corner of the room with a gun between their legs, ready to pounce should Henri misbehave.

As they climbed up the stairs to the old couple's apartment, Nell said wearily, 'Oh well, let's visit the old womaniser.'

Jeanne wondered what a womaniser looked like. Would he be wearing a silk dressing gown and holding a long cigarette holder? In fact, all she saw was an old man with a plaid shawl round his shoulders to keep out the cold. Tante Marie was welcoming and sweet as usual.

Jeanne asked to see Oncle Henri's paintings, but he said they were up in the studio and it was too cold to go up there. If she came back in the summer he would take her up there to see them. It never came about. He died soon afterwards.

19. The Reunion

Back at the British Embassy, the official had news at last. 'Mrs Sarginson, please present yourselves here tomorrow morning early, with your luggage. We may be able to transport you to England.'

That afternoon, Nell, making enquiries at the Post Office, found it was now possible to send telegrams to England. She sent one to Tom, saying, 'With Gaston. Our reunion 20 Kisses.' A telegram arrived from Tom by return: 'Overjoyed with your telegram. We understand you are arriving 20 December. Love.' The lack of punctuation in Nell's telegram had caused him to question whether she was sending him 20 kisses, or whether they were in fact arriving on the 20th!

But they had reckoned without the fog. Each morning, Gaston and Hortense waved goodbye from the windows of their flat and Nell and the girls, carrying all they possessed, went by Metro to the British Embassy and sat around all day. Then an announcement would be made: 'We regret, ladies and gentlemen, we are unable to repatriate you today, due to foggy conditions prevailing over the Channel. Please present yourselves early tomorrow . . .' etc. Nell and the girls would return to the flat to be welcomed back by the old couple. This performance went on for several days, and Christmas drew ever nearer.

On December 23rd, the official had good news. 'Ladies and gentlemen, the fog has thinned somewhat over the Channel, and we are hoping for a takeoff. We shall transport you to the airport, but nevertheless, may still be unable to fly you to England today. It depends on the weather report.'

Excited, they boarded an RAF lorry, together with the other lucky repatriates and were driven to Le Bourget airport. While they waited, they were handed RAF identification tags, which they had to tie on to their clothes and each item in their possession. Marie grinned. 'It doesn't make you feel too confident about the flight, does it?'

As they walked out onto the tarmac towards the Royal Canadian Air Force Dakota, standing with its engine revving, Marie couldn't resist saying out of the corner of her month, 'Well, I hope the elastic doesn't break!'

They stepped up a rickety gangway and climbed aboard. Used for paratroopers, it had long wooden benches down each side facing each other. Jeanne sat down gingerly and noticed an old French lady opposite, dressed entirely in black. She sat erect with her back straight and held a cake box in one hand and a bunch of flowers in the other. She didn't flinch once during the entire journey.

An RAF officer came aboard, checking the passengers.

'We may yet have to turn back if the fog thickens. Anyway, we'll take off and see how we go. Wizard show!' he said and disappeared.

As the plane taxied and took off, Jeanne, who had never flown before and hadn't known quite what to expect, thought the plane felt quite unsafe. Outside, the thin fog swirled around giving off an eerie glow. She wondered just how old the plane was. As they took to the air, the flight was noisy, draughty, shaky and turbulent. Midway across the Channel, the plane lurched suddenly and dropped about ten feet before righting itself and regaining its composure. But Jeanne felt as though she had left her stomach behind. This happened two or three times and she felt sick.

As a distraction she looked out of the window and, far below, saw the angry, uninviting, wintry sea with 'white horses' riding the waves.

This was nothing like flying was in the films, Jeanne thought. There was no smart, uniformed steward bringing trays full of delicious concoctions in ice-clinking glasses. She felt quite disappointed. It was not pleasant at all. She couldn't imagine why she had looked forward to the flight.

Just when she thought she was really going to be sick, she looked down, and there, through a gap in the fog, were the white cliffs of the south of England.

'Look, look!' she shouted. 'There it is! Is that it? It's England . . . we're here!' There was a faint cheer from the passengers. It had been a rough journey.

They landed at Croydon airport and were taken to a reception lounge. An RAF medical officer walked up and down and talked to the tired passengers, checking them over, looking for signs of disease or neglect. He stood in front of Jeanne, now recovering from her nausea in a comfortable armchair. There was concern in his eyes. 'And how old are you?'

Jeanne, summoning up her best English, said, 'Half past twelve.'

The MO threw back his head and roared with laughter, and people around joined in. Jeanne was puzzled. What were they laughing at? She had thought her English was rather good.

They were driven into London by coach with a huge, orange winter sun on the horizon line silhouetting the bare trees. The coach stopped outside a building and they stepped out in a daze. They had no idea where they were. Inside, a glorious sight awaited them. Smiling ladies, all in twin-sets and pearls, led them through into a large sitting room where a log fire sparkled merrily. There were Christmas cards on the mantelpiece, and in a corner stood a beautiful Christmas tree.

Nell surveyed the scene. 'Well, this is an improvement on the Paris dosshouse, and no mistake!'

Jeanne went up to the decorated tree, touching the baubles and the sparkling streamers. It was unlike other Christmas trees she'd seen, not like a French Christmas tree. It was gaudy, more fun, and quite unlike the one the German soldiers had so simply decorated back in the church in Cambrai, all that time ago. She wondered whether Christmas trees have different nationalities, just like people, and talk different languages to each other.

The Smiling Ladies brought trays of tea and fruitcake and the travellers, warming themselves by the cheerful fire, began to relax and to forget the awful plane journey. Leaflets were handed out informing them that they were at Rochester Row Rest Centre in Victoria. It told them how to apply for identity cards, ration books, clothing coupons, gas masks, etc. The war wasn't over yet.

Jeanne didn't remember much after that. She was so tired.

The next morning, they were each given a thorough medical check-up. The doctor checked for signs of infectious diseases as well as their health in general. When they were given a clean bill of health, they were free to leave.

At the reception desk, they were given travel vouchers. As they were about to leave, Nell did the most extraordinary thing. She fished deep into the contents of her handbag, among her papers and, pulling out a one pound note, asked sweetly, 'Are these still in use?' The Smiling Ladies behind the desk smiled and nodded. Nell folded and pushed the one pound note through the slit in the top of the collection box. 'I wouldn't want anyone to think we were charity cases!' she said to the girls. Through all the long years of hardship, she had held on to that one pound note. It must have been a symbol to her. She probably felt that, as long as she still had it, she'd get safely back home to England some day, somehow.

At Euston station they boarded the train for Birmingham. Jeanne was taking everything in, so many things were different – the way people dressed, the buildings, the hoardings, the double-decker buses – especially the double-decker buses. And Nell's chic Parisian beret, with a feather on the side, so much admired by the girls when she had bought it back in Cambrai, now looked totally out of place. Nell was quite definitely overdressed.

They settled in a railway carriage and waited to leave. The guard blew a whistle and waved a green flag. They were off!

The carriage was stuffy. The upholstery smelled of a combination of engine smoke and stale cigarette smoke. Above the seats were pre-war sepia photographs of seaside resorts that could be reached by rail – Llandudno, Skegness, Scarborough. Jeanne didn't think any of them looked worth visiting, they looked so depressing, but maybe, she decided, it was the photographer's fault and the towns weren't all that bad really.

Under the seats were pipes, pumping hot air into the carriage and creating an unhealthy fug. Nell decided she could do with a little air. She opened the window, and smoke and smuts came pouring in, covering her with tiny black specs. She promptly closed it again, deciding she'd rather stifle.

Jeanne resumed her favourite place by the window. Coming out of London, there were the same scenes of bombing and devastation, just as there had been on the Paris outskirts. Near the railway line she could see houses with windows criss-crossed with thick brown tape. This was to protect the occupants. Should they be bombed, they would not be injured by flying glass.

Then, gradually, the houses grew thinner and thinner, and they were in the country. But there were no flat fields, as she had been used to in northern France, but small fields, surrounded by hedges. Pretty and different, not at all what she had been expecting. Well, she didn't know what she had been expecting, but the English countryside was quite a surprise to her.

This was England, the promised land . . . the land of plenty. Well . . . the land of plenty of rationing at least! Jeanne went over to sit down next to Nell, and in the fuggy heat and the repetitive rhythm of the wheels on the rails, *da-da-da-da, da-da-da-da*, she fell asleep. She was so tired.

She was awakened by a voice, shouting out, 'Birmingham . . . Snow Hill, Birmingham.' They were here, they had arrived. Before the train had stopped, the three girls were up at the carriage door, struggling and fighting, each one wanting to be the first to see Tom.

One of them, either Marie or Irene, shouted, 'There he is! There he is!' Jeanne never knew which one.

At the end of the platform was a small group of people, and Tom in front, tears streaming down his face, holding a huge bunch of white chrysanthemums. Jeanne held back shyly for a few seconds as the others went to him, shouting, kissing and hugging. Then she ran along the platform and hurled herself at him. 'Papa! Daddy, Daddy!'

1944 – Present

20. What Happened Next

When they arrived at 6 Oxford Road, they found that Mrs Reeves, Aunt Rikkie's housekeeper, had prepared a lavish tea. Jeanne could hardly believe her eyes. There were delicate tinned salmon and cucumber and egg and cress sandwiches, tinned peaches with condensed milk, a Victoria sponge, a trifle made in Rikkie's special trifle bowl, and, most surprising of all, jelly of an indescribable green colour in dainty glass dishes. Jeanne couldn't remember ever having jelly. This was the land of plenty, she thought. They were back, and every day would be like this.

Christmas came and went in a happy haze, there was so much to talk about and catch up on.

What Jeanne didn't realise was that Rikkie and Gramp had saved as much as they could from their meagre rations and that, as Rikkie was PA to the Regional Director of the BBC, Percy Edgar, she had begged, borrowed or stolen what she could from the BBC canteen. The family were soon to find out how things really were.

When the ration books arrived, Jeanne was sent to Sadie's Sweetshop around the corner to get the sweet rations for five people. She came back with nearly a shoebox full of the most beautiful foreign-looking sweets. She couldn't wait to get her hands on them. Jeanne remembered how in occupied Cambrai, where no sweets were to be had, she would stop off at the Boulangerie and get fifty centimes worth of yeast and walk slowly home, dipping her fingers in and relishing it. The Baker's wife had asked if it was for her, and when she said yes, looked at her pityingly. The shoebox of sweets was put away in the wardrobe, to be brought out on special occasions. But Jeanne couldn't contain herself. She would sneak upstairs and help herself to one or two, and eventually a whole handful, and caused a minor family scandal when Nell found the box empty, but it had just been too great a temptation for Jeanne. She had eaten a whole month's sweet ration for five people.

Nell, like so many women, had learned to fend for herself during the war, and now found herself relegated to her father's kitchen, housekeeper to seven people. Her vision of England being the land of milk and honey quickly faded. Her beautiful Parisian beret with a feather in it landed at the back of the wardrobe and, together with the ever-reliable Mrs Reeves, she found herself wrestling a different set of ration books and rules. Gone were the tender days of coffee and brandy with Emil in the afternoons; they had to be forgotten. She donned a pinny and didn't take it off for the next twenty years.

Tom was back working for Courtaulds Textiles. He had been interviewed by his bosses several times when he came back to England. 'I had to prove to them I hadn't gone crackers!' he said, laughing. He became a sort of troubleshooter: first sent to the Preston factory, then to help with the opening of the new firm in Carrickfergus in Northern Ireland. He was offered his old job back in Calais and, as soon as he was able, he returned there. He stayed three months, but found it impossible to obtain equipment and get the firm re-started; it was one long frustration. He decided he would be safer in England. He applied to return, sold the car and came back. 'Anyway,' he said, 'France is moribund.'

So Courtaulds Textiles offered him the post of Chief Electrician in Coventry, which he gratefully accepted. He was a bitter man, difficult to live with. The best years of his life had been wasted by two wars, years that could not be recaptured, and the wonderful times he had dreamed of while in internment camp did not materialize. Post-war Britain was a very grim place. Rationing and shortages carried on for a long time.

Marie immediately applied to join the WRENS. When she enlisted, she spent the whole morning strutting around the house, waving her papers in the air, and singing:

> *'We joined the Navy*
> *To see the world*
> *And what did we see*
> *We saw the sea.'*

Tom was sorry to see his beautiful, lively girl leave so soon. He had hoped they would spend time together so that he would get to know her.

Irene's wonderful French classical education was of no use in England. There had been talk of her becoming a doctor but she opted to be a probationary nurse at Birmingham General Hospital and started there at the age of seventeen.

Jeanne, meanwhile, was making friends. Nell told her that a French lady and her daughter lived down the road at Number 44. Jeanne became a regular visitor, delighted to be able to speak French, and the daughter, Josette, and Jeanne hit it off right away and have remained friends ever since.

Next door to Number 6 lived two boys, Philip and Christopher (known as Kipper). They lent Jeanne their old books and she learnt to read English with Nell's help, following Noddy and Big Ears' adventures and the joys of boating and fishing in old Ladybird books. Her name had been put down for St Joseph's Convent School in Acock's Green to start school the following September and she had a lot of work to do to catch up with girls of her age.

Philip appeared to have a tick, constantly swinging his right arm from his back to his front, keeping it straight the whole time. This puzzled Jeanne who wondered what on earth he was doing. It was strange behaviour and it wasn't something French boys did. All became clear when they played cricket together with a crowd of friends in the fields at the back. He'd been practising his bowling action! Jeanne had no idea what was going on, as cricket wasn't played in France, but once she caught on she was quite happy just to be a fielder.

The boys had another strange ritual. One of them would say, 'Quick, quick, it's nearly time for the 4.05 London to Edinburgh,' and they would all run down to the fence alongside the railway. As the train rushed by they'd say, pointing to the plaque on the side of the monster, 'It's a namer, look, it's a namer! It's King George the fifth!' and they would cross the name out in the little book they were holding. Another would say in a derisory way, 'Oh I've got that one, I've had it ages.' Occasionally, an LNER (London & North-Eastern Railway) locomotive would pass by on loan to the LMS (London Midland Scottish Railway). The boys booed and jeered.

Her new friends seemed so much younger than children back in France. Nicole had started hanging around with the boys, Jeanne following a few steps behind. How very different life was here, she thought. Here she played cricket and collected train numbers. She felt as though she was ten again.

One day, Aunt Rikkie said she had a treat for Jeanne, who didn't know whether to be pleased or sorry. She had no idea what a treat was! Then it was explained to her that Rikkie had four complimentary tickets for Cinderella at Birmingham's Alexandra Theatre. So Jeanne saw her first pantomime at the age of twelve and three quarters, and enjoyed every minute of it. Things were decidedly looking up.

Towards the start of May, it was obvious that the war was coming to an end. There was excitement in the air, you could almost smell it; and when the announcement was made that the war was over, May the 8th was declared VE Day (Victory in Europe Day) and the whole of the world erupted. 'Thank God, thank God it's all over, peace at last, they'll be home!' Everyone had a smile on their face, and strangers talked to each other, laughing with relief and delight. At last, the men would come home and pick their lives up where they had left off and everything would be back to normal.

The celebrations were still going on two days later when Jeanne celebrated her thirteenth birthday. A party was held for her at Number 6. Josette, Philip and Kipper brought presents for her. She was so excited. 'Imagine . . . presents . . .' she said, '. . .for me!' Rikkie had again twisted someone's arm at the BBC canteen, and a beautiful birthday cake covered with a red, white and blue icing Union Jack was in the centre of the table, waiting to be shared out. Candles were lit and Jeanne blew them out. Then everyone – Mum, Dad, Gramp, Rikkie, Josette, Philip and Kipper – sang *Happy Birthday*. It was just wonderful. Jeanne felt very special, like a princess. And she had a feeling that things were going to be all right.

Epilogue

Returning to places you knew in your childhood and seeing them with a grown-up's eyes, makes things seem so very different.

I returned to the house of my birth in Calais quite recently. We were very kindly welcomed by the present occupiers and sat in their garden, what had been my wonderful garden where I had played in with my dog Dick and the beautiful cat Zezette. It is still a large garden, but the house seemed so small now, tiny, and yet it had been my huge castle up to the age of eight. How the memory plays tricks.

My sister Irene and I visited Tante Suzanne about thirty years ago. She was my father's cousin in Paris. I now realised that she lived in the choicest part of intellectual Paris, that the church opposite her flat was the renowned Church of St Germain des Pres and the café opposite was Les Deux Magots, mentioned as *the* meeting place of all Bohemian

Paris of the sixties. The walls of her flat were covered with her father's paintings, as well as hers, and the beautifully carved furniture had been made by her grandfather, who had been a cabinet maker.

Some time later, we heard from a Madame France Fremaux, who was Suzanne's godchild, that Suzanne had died. She had been in her nineties and very frail. France Fremaux had been left with a problem: Suzanne had stipulated in her will that her dying wish was to be buried in the vault of Marguerite Castelle, which is our family vault in the Cimetiere de Montparnasse. All our deceased ancestors lie there. It turned out that the vault was already full, and if Suzanne were to be buried there, the coffin of a long dead relative would have to be removed from the vault and buried elsewhere in the cemetery.

Suzanne's solicitor, Maitre Charles Bricard, requested that all persons having the right to the vault give permission for the coffin of a dead relative be removed and for Suzanne to be interred there, but it had to be done within a year. Meanwhile, Suzanne had been temporarily buried elsewhere. My sister Irene, her son John, my three daughters, Julie, Marina and Sophie and I had to send a letter authorising France Fremaux to have the vault opened, explaining our right of parentage, a copy of our birth certificate and other proof of identity. Irene and I decided not to bother my sister Marie's children; she had died some time before and we thought that the link with them was broken. After several months, with all the paper work done, one of our unknown relatives was disturbed from their eternal sleep and buried elsewhere; Suzanne's coffin was exhumed and at last placed in the family vault, as she wished. A very French story!

I have been back to Cambrai in northern France a couple of times. It's now a thriving town, proud of itself and looking as though it has forgotten the horrors of two world wars. When I stand on the main square and look at the Flemish-style hotels, I still see them covered with red and black flags embellished with swastikas. I just cannot forget.

Walking down to the old dilapidated quarter where we lived, I was amazed to find that the whole district is now a preservation area, and that the council is erecting plaques on each street corner pointing out items of interest to visitors. I knocked on the door of number 8, rue de Monstrelet where we lived for three years, but there was no reply. I had the feeling that it was social housing and that visitors would be unwelcome. I wonder if the smelly toilet is still in the yard, or has it now pride of place in a local museum?

We returned to Rieux-en-Cambresis in 2010, laid some flowers at the memorial to the massacre of September 2nd 1944, then drove down to 15, Rue de la Gare, where we had stayed for a few months to get away from the bombings. While taking photos a man approached us. He was painting the house next door and it turned out he was Camille Jackemin, whom I used to play with! We were told off one time by his father for running in his asparagus patch and knocking the tips off. Camille invited us into his kitchen, introduced us to his wife, and we had a coffee and reminisced.

We had an appointment with Monsieur Moussi, the mayor of Rieux-en-Cambresis, and his deputy at the Town Hall. We had asked if we could meet anyone who had been in the village on the day of the massacre. We met Jean Devaux, who had been working in his father's fields that day and had witnessed the whole thing. He described how he had laid flat in the field and hidden, terrified, when he'd seen the German armoured vehicle approaching and stopping. He'd watched in frozen horror as, one by one, his friends, mostly his school friends, had been mown down. That evening, he had gone with the family ox and cart and brought some of the bodies back to the village. We talked and it brought back the whole, awful episode. Monsieur Moussi presented us with an ashtray embossed with the Rieux-en-Cambresis coat of arms and a book published by Lille University, which is a study of the Rieux dialect – fast disappearing no doubt. We took more photos and left.

My friend Claudette and her husband Daniel are still in Rieux-en-Cambresis. We have kept in touch over the years. We had a long-standing invitation and stayed with them for a few days last year. They live in a large double-fronted house right in the village centre. Daniel explained how their present sitting room had once been a shop and workshop owned by his parents selling overalls and work clothes, including the *bleu-de-travail*, the blue overalls traditionally worn by French labourers and workmen. The clothes were made by several seamstresses in a workshop in the garden. The workshop has now been dismantled, and Daniel, a retired dentist, is enjoying growing his vegetables on the patch where the workshop used to be.

Looking out of the window onto the street, Claudette pointed out the wall opposite, pockmarked with hundred-year-old shell holes. She said her grandfather had been the village policeman during World War One. Rieux-en-Cambresis was occupied, but right on the front line. Her grandfather and another man had been sending messages by carrier pigeon denoting troop movements when they had been caught and shot by the Germans.

This whole area of northern France was given over to producing textiles until the sixties. There was a textile factory in the village producing particularly fine products. Claudette used to buy seconds from the factory, and she showed me a sheet she had bought, part of Catherine Deneuve, the film actress's wedding trousseau. It was made of the finest of fine cottons with small pink hearts on it. She said the same firm had also made a long ceremonial tablecloth for the Shah of Iran, covered in embroidery and interwoven with gold thread. All that is gone now, and it seems on the whole that there is no local employment for the people of Rieux-en-Cambresis and they have to find work in Cambrai.

After a few days with our friends we left, promising to return. The constant pull to return to the country of my birth never fades.

Acknowledgements

Thanks to my husband Tony and my own three daughters, Julie, Sophie and especially Marina; to my sister Irene and my sister Marie's memory; to First Paragraph creative writing group in Bristol for showing me how to get started and to Myrmidon for seeing the potential in my writing.

MORE GREAT READS FROM MYRMIDON

Queen of Bedlam

Laura Purcell

London 1788 . . .

The calm order of Queen Charlotte's court is shattered by screams. The King of England is going mad.

Left alone with thirteen children and with the country on the brink of war, Charlotte has to fight to hold her husband's throne. It is a time of unrest and revolution but most of all Charlotte fears the King himself, someone she can no longer love or trust. She has lost her marriage to madness and there is nothing she can do other than continue to fulfil her royal duty.

Her six daughters are desperate to escape their palace asylum. Their only hope lies in a good marriage, but no prince wants the daughter of a madman. They are forced to take love wherever they find it – with devastating consequences.

The moving, true story of George III's madness and the women whose lives it destroyed.

". . . a masterfully written and well-researched novel written by someone who has truly mastered the craft of evoking readers' emotions."
Historical Novel Society

ISBN: 978-1-910183-01-4   Price: £8.99
AVAILABLE AS AN E-BOOK

Hope Against Hope
Sally Zigmond

Yorkshire, 1838 . . .

At the dawn of the Victorian epoch two young sisters, stoical and industrious Carrie and carefree and vivacious May, lose home and livelihood when their Leeds pub is sold out from under them to make way for the coming of the railway. They head for Harrogate to find work in the spa town's burgeoning hotel trade only to fall prey to fraudsters and predators before being driven apart by misunderstanding, pride and a mutual sense of betrayal.

Estranged from one another, Carrie and May must each pursue their own destinies as they seek to overcome misfortune and look for love and lasting happiness. Their separate paths will cross those of three men: Alex Sinclair, a bold and warm-spirited Scottish railway pioneer; Charles Hammond, the dissolute and tormented heir to a wealthy and manipulative mother, and Byron Taylor, a ruthless entrepreneur and consummate womaniser.

Populated by a host of engaging characters and by turns poignant, warm and humorous, *Hope Against Hope* is compelling tale of triumph, love and redemption that takes us on a ten-year journey through the salons and bordellos of Harrogate, the cholera infected slums of Leeds and the bloody streets of revolutionary Paris.

ISBN: 978-1-905802-19-7   Price: £8.99
AVAILABLE AS AN E-BOOK

Mrs Lincoln

Janis Cooke Newman

(May 20ᵗʰ)
Mrs Mary Lincoln admitted today – from Chicago – Age 56 – Widow of ex-President Lincoln – declared insane by the Cook County Court May 19ᵗʰ – 1875.

Patient Progress Reports for Bellevue Place Sanatorium.
Incarcerated in an insane asylum after committal proceedings instigated by her own son, Mary Lincoln resolves to tell her own story in order to preserve and prove her own sanity and secure her release. But can she succeed?

". . . this epic drama exerts an exceptional pull . . . an impressive, engrossing and moving piece of historical imagining and characterisation."   Holly Kyte, *The Sunday Telegraph*

". . . a tender and thoughtful portrait of a 19ᵗʰ century woman severely misunderstood... *Mrs Lincoln* unfolds with plenty to inspire and is all the more poignant for a timely arrival."
                                        Sarah Emily Miano, *The Times*

"As I read it, I wept. I cannot recommend a book more. Mary is a very powerful novel."
Pat Schroeder, *President of the Association of American Publishers*

ISBN: 978-1-905802-21-0   Price £8.99

Searing and achingly beautiful of Sub-Saharan West Africa ...

Harmattan
Gavin Weston

Haoua is a young girl growing up in a remote village in the Republic of Niger. Spirited and intelligent, she has benefited from a stable home life and a loving and attentive mother and enjoys working and playing with her siblings and friends.

She worships her elder brother, Abdelkrim, a serving soldier who sends money home to support the family. But on his last home visit, Abdelkrim quarrels with their father, accusing him of gambling away the money he sends and being the cause of their mother's worsening health. It also emerges that their father plans to take a second wife.

Despite this Haoua finds contentment in her schoolwork, her dreams of becoming a teacher and in writing assiduously to the family in Ireland who act as her aid sponsors.

But for Haoua, there are new storm clouds on the horizon: as civil strife mounts in Niger, she fears for Abdelkrim's safety, her mother's illness is much more serious than anyone had recognised, and her father's plans are turning out to be far more threatening than she could have ever imagined.

Approaching her twelfth birthday, Haoua feels alone and vulnerable for the very first time in her life.

ISBN: 978-1-905802-75-3   Price: £8.99
AVAILABLE AS AN E-BOOK